TAEKWONDO

TAEKWONDO

A step-by-step guide to the Korean art of self-defence

Master Kevin Hornsey

6TH DAN WTF
Olympic Referee

Photography by Laura Knox

CONNECTIONS
BOOK PUBLISHING

I would like to dedicate this book to my wife, Lindsay, and my children, Rebecca and Jessica. The most important people in my life.

A CONNECTIONS EDITION

This edition published in Great Britain in 2002 by
Connections Book Publishing Limited
St Chad's House, 148 King's Cross Road
London WC1X 9DH

British Library Cataloguing-in-Publication data available on request.

ISBN 1-85906-100-1

10 9 8 7 6 5 4 3 2 1

Phototypeset in Sabon MT and Humanist 777 BT using QuarkXPress on Apple Macintosh
Origination by Pixel Graphics, Singapore
Printed by Star Standard Industries (PTE Ltd), Singapore

Contents

Foreword by Dr KIM Un Yong   6
President of the World Taekwondo Federation

Part one
Introducing Taekwondo   9

Part two
Training   27

    Warming up   32
    Basic techniques   42
       Stances   46
       Punching   50
       Blocking   54
       Striking   66
       Kicking   78
    Poomsae   90

Part three
Taking it further   115

    Sparring   116
    Self-defence   132
    Breaking   136

Glossary   140
Resources   141
Index   142
Acknowledgements   144

Foreword · *Dr KIM Un Yong*

I would like to congratulate Mr Hornsey on the publication of his book on Taekwondo, a book aimed at giving learners a step-by-step guide to the Korean martial art. As a young Taekwondoist, his devotion to the promotion of the sport deserves the highest praise, for which I am at a loss for words.

I would not hesitate to call Mr Hornsey an ambassador of Taekwondo in Britain. He has long been devoted to the dissemination of the martial art, not only as a competitor but also as an instructor in his country. I am well aware of the difficulties of publishing, as I have also published several books. I express my special gratitude to, and respect for, Mr Hornsey for his authorship.

Taekwondo is not merely a physical discipline for self-defence: rather, it is a physical and mental skill that combines and incorporates Korean virtues and spiritual characteristics peculiar to the Orient. I think the publication of a book on Taekwondo not only publicizes the martial art, but also introduces the Oriental culture to Western society. In turn, the sharing of cultures contributes greatly to enhancing a mutual understanding between the people of East and West. It also helps expedite the internationalization of Taekwondo in the truest sense.

The exceptional development of Taekwondo, which has achieved successful transformation from a local martial art to an Olympic sport practised by more than fifty million people in some 168 countries, would not have been possible without unceasing effort by all Taekwondo enthusiasts, like Mr Hornsey, across the world.

The existence of people like Mr Hornsey gives me a sense of confidence that the future of our sport is bright. I would also like to extend my deepest gratitude to him on behalf of all lovers of Taekwondo.

DR KIM UN YONG
PRESIDENT
THE WORLD TAEKWONDO FEDERATION

Part one
Introducing Taekwondo

Here, I offer my insight for those who are about to embark on the Taekwondo journey. This section introduces the fundamentals, from explaining what Taekwondo is and the benefits it offers, through to finding a reputable dojang (place of training) and preparing for your first lessons. As any martial artist will tell you, your knowledge at this stage will guide you onto the right path and shape your future experiences. Take careful note and decide well, having made this first – and life-changing – decision to embrace this beautiful art that is Taekwondo.

Taekwondo *A brief history*

It is widely published that the martial arts have existed since ancient times as a means of self-defence, recreation and complete body and mind exercise. Many cave paintings exist in various archaeological sites throughout Asia that bear out this well-documented fact. Korea is rich in such historical sites, with numerous murals depicting ancient warriors in typical martial-art postures to be found decorating caves and tombs that have been uncovered by excavation teams over the course of the last century.

The earliest martial-art forms in Korea possessed different names according to the different regions of the time, and these names were handed down through the generations to modern times. It was not until Korea's liberation from Japanese rule in 1945 that these arts, practised largely in secret during this period, were to enjoy a revival as the people sought to reaffirm their national identity. Through the popularity of the respective disciplines, the different skills of the various styles rapidly became more widely known and practised. This, together

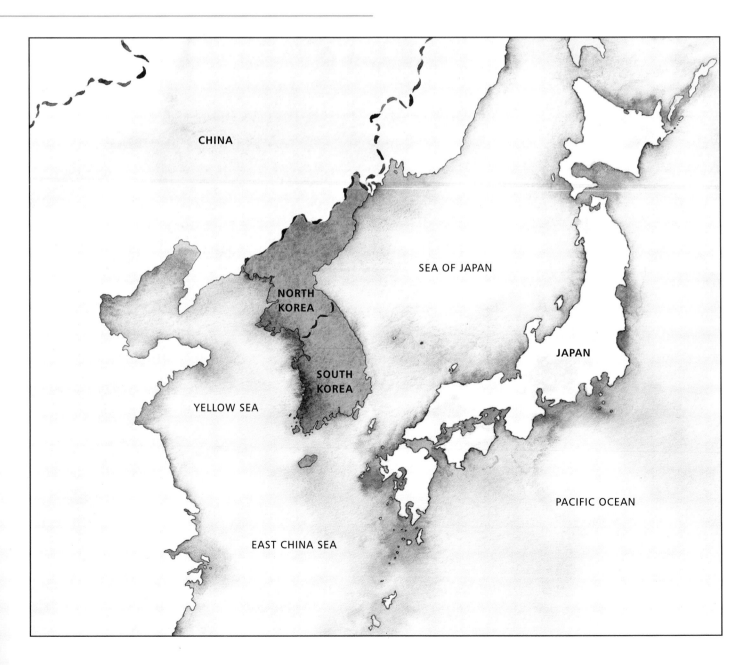

NOTABLE ACHIEVEMENTS

- **1975** Affiliation of WTF to the General Assembly of International Sports Federations (GAISF).

- **1976** Adoption of Taekwondo into the World Military Championships by the International Military Sports Council (CISM).

- **1980** The International Olympic Committee (IOC) recognizes WTF at its 83rd session in Moscow.

- **1981** Affiliation of WTF to the International Council of Sports Science & Physical Education (ICSSPE).

- **1986** The Federation International du Sport Universitaire (FISU) adopts Taekwondo as an event for the World University Championships.

- **1988** Taekwondo competition features as an exhibition sport at the 24th Olympic Games in Seoul, Korea.

- **1991** Goodwill Games Inc. adopts Taekwondo as an official sport at the 3rd World Games.

- **1994** Taekwondo is adopted as a full participating sport of the Sydney 2000 Olympic Games.

- **1998** The General Assembly of the Supreme Council of Sports in Africa (SCSA) resolves to include Taekwondo in the official programme of the 7th All African Games.

- **2000** The International Olympic Committee confirms Taekwondo as an Olympic sport for the Athens 2004 Olympic Games.

- **2002** WTF moves its offices to downtown Seoul after 30 years' location at the Kukkiwon, since its foundation. Membership of WTF rises to 168 nations.

with the cooperation of the Masters of these arts, paved the way for the collective name of 'Taekwondo' to be adopted formally in 1965.

THE RISE OF TAEKWONDO

A few short years later, as Taekwondo spread around the globe, it became necessary to acknowledge its internationalization, and so – under the direct supervision of Dr KIM Un Yong, President of the newly formed Korea Taekwondo Association – the world Taekwondo headquarters (*Kukkiwon*) was built in Seoul, Korea. Shortly after, on 28 May 1973, representatives from the thirty-five practising nations came together to form the World Taekwondo Federation (WTF).

Since then, Taekwondo has enjoyed an unparalleled rise in growth and recognition, with many extraordinary achievements in its latter-day existence (see left).

A GLOBAL JOURNEY

Now, with over fifty million practitioners worldwide, Taekwondo is truly a global sport. From the smallest village halls in some of the most underprivileged townships of the world, to national sports arenas in the largest cities, Taekwondo can be seen being practised and enjoyed by children from as young as five years old, to grandparents well into their senior years.

Your journey into Taekwondo may begin right here. Savour every moment of it as you travel along its path, for you will not know where it may lead you until you take the first steps.

Why choose Taekwondo?

People are universally drawn to Taekwondo for a variety of reasons, whether it be as a practical means of self-defence, an effective method of developing and maintaining a high level of physical stamina, a way of achieving a greater sense of self-discipline and control, or as a system of increasing and focusing powers of concentration. Taekwondo has a great deal to offer all of us, whatever our age or level of ability.

WHAT IS TAEKWONDO?

Described by many as 'action philosophy', Taekwondo is the Korean art of self-defence. Literally translated, *tae* means 'foot', *kwon* means 'fist' and *do* means 'art'. It is, however, far more than just a fancy form of kicking and punching. It is designed to cultivate a person into having a strong moral conscience through physical training, mental guidance and philosophical values. More than just a system of bodily exercise, Taekwondo is also a way of life.

It includes the physical practice of a wide variety of movements – movements that have been devised into a complete system of combat self-defence, involving attacking and defending through blocking, stepping, jumping, punching, striking and kicking techniques. Some of the movements are soft, while others are hard, sometimes performed slowly, sometimes fast, but – when done properly – always effective.

EVERYDAY BENEFITS

Through regular and sustained practice, the Taekwondo student can develop many physical attributes that will prove to be useful in everyday life. You will benefit from better coordination, increased flexibility, improved cardiovascular conditioning and added strength. In addition, in the pursuance of physical mastery of these techniques, one cannot be entirely successful without also developing very positive mental disciplines along the way. Through correct training, you can build

THE TAEKWONDO TENETS

Through its practice, you will learn the most important tenets of Taekwondo:

- Etiquette
- Modesty
- Perseverance
- Self-control
- Indomitable spirit

true self-confidence, gain better judgement and improve your self-control.

While developing these physical and mental qualities, your studies will inevitably expose you to many of the valuable philosophical lessons offered by Taekwondo. Among these lessons are the meaning of modesty, courtesy, loyalty, humility, trust, and respect for others. By building these virtues into your life through the practice of Taekwondo, you will promote a sense of peace, health and happiness. In time you will feel stronger yet calmer, emphatic while at the same time benevolent. Adding these qualities to the ones you already possess will enhance the positive aspects of your character and help you to improve the balance between spirit and body.

Taekwondo philosophy emphasizes the good that exists in humanity. Through exercising its principles, you will begin to see challenges where you might previously have seen only problems. You will also begin to appreciate that you are capable of extraordinary achievements, and will become familiar with rewarding yourself with success from your efforts, when you would otherwise have resigned yourself to defeat.

UNIVERSAL TAEKWONDO

Taekwondo truly is for everyone. What began as an exclusive and little-known Oriental martial art has grown into a global sport which emphasizes strong mental discipline and physical excellence. Taekwondo is regarded as being the most effective, practical, sensible, no-nonsense self-defence system, and I agree wholeheartedly with my fellow Masters that it is the greatest martial art in the world.

TAKING THE CHALLENGE

When I was first approached to write this book, I immediately saw a challenge. As an instructor with over thirty years' experience, I knew that if I could present a logical and easy-to-understand supplement to a student's in-class training programme, then their experience and understanding of Taekwondo would surely be all the better for it. It was a great opportunity for me to make a further contribution to a much wider audience than my direct contact with my own club members and those that I teach allows me.

Needless to say, I took up the challenge in true Taekwondo spirit and tradition. For, as I think back to the day that I stepped into the training hall as a young boy to experience my first lesson, I felt exactly the same sense of foreboding and uncertainty about what might be the outcome. And so, besides what my instructor introduced me to during that first class, the most significant lesson that I took from Taekwondo was that very often your biggest adversary is not the assailant standing before you, but apprehension from within you, and fear of the unknown. It is this that so often stands between us and the achievement of our desires. As human beings, we are capable of so much more than we know, if only we are bold enough to face down our fears and say 'yes' to the challenge.

LESSONS OFFERED

Taekwondo offers many such lessons, no matter why you may choose to enrol. From your very first class you will be introduced to a code of conduct and ethical virtues that may initially seem quite strange. You will be expected to comply with new rules and principles that will ensure order and discipline in the *dojang* (place of training). This code is essential to promoting a safe and responsible environment and attitude, and cultivating the appropriate behaviour of those who learn this wonderful martial art called Taekwondo.

The moment one enters or leaves the dojang, or faces the instructor or partner for practice, the junior member bows as a salutation and show of respect to the senior. Not enough is written or understood of the significance of the bow. It is a demonstration of regard and humility that is mutually significant, as the senior member will immediately – and always – bow in return. Such a courtesy, performed with sincerity, fosters a spirit of trust, loyalty and cooperation that is rarely seen in other walks of life, and which engenders a greater sense of respect for oneself and others (see page 19 for more on the bow).

From this simple yet meaningful act, we are also reminded of our position and order within the group structure: just as we bow both before and after receiving instruction, so, as seniors – by observing this tradition – we are reminded of our duty to share our knowledge and experience to help and improve our fellow trainees. Such unfamiliar principles will soon become normal to you, and by living them you will grow to become strong in character, gentle in temperament, modest in victory and humble in defeat.

Spirit

The spirit of Taekwondo cannot be found simply by observing the remarkable physical accomplishments of the skilled practitioner. No, the true spirit of the art lies in the experience gained through the combined pursuance of both mind and body to the goal of attaining mastery through those skills and philosophical values of one's own inborn capability.

Only through dedication, self-sacrifice and single-minded focus can one hope to achieve all that Taekwondo offers. To realize our full potential requires us to unite the extraordinary powers of body and mind so that they function as one in total harmony. This, I truly believe, is our formula for triumph in life. Whatever our aims, success must not be left to chance, for this is the view of the under-achiever.

During my many travels throughout the world, I remember well one of the lessons I learned as a young 1st Dan visiting the dojang of an esteemed Taekwondo Grand Master. On this very subject he observed that, in terms of the inner power – or spirit – that we all possess, though humanity may be physically rich, we often remain spiritually poor. Those words have been firmly imprinted in my mind since then, and have served me well as a driving force in my desire to achieve my goals. Although the Taekwondo path is not the only route to a more harmonious life and peaceful co-existence, it is certainly one that is embraced and cherished by an ever-increasing number of people in societies the world over.

Mount Taedunsan, Korea. The majestic landscape evokes the spirit – the inner power and beauty – of this great Korean martial art.

Finding a dojang

The art of Taekwondo has many facets, any number of which will draw interest from a wide cross-section of people from all aspects of any given community. But where do you start?

FIRST STEPS

Taekwondo is hugely popular around the world, so you should have no difficulty finding a class – or dojang – somewhere in your area. The dojang is the place where students come together to learn Taekwondo, and it is vital that you try to find one that is suitable for your training requirements and which will satisfy your own personal expectations. Check the newspapers or the internet, or contact your National Olympic Association for the address or contact number of the recognized governing federation in your country, and then give them a call for more information. They will be able to direct you to a locally recognized school or club. (See also *Resources* on page 141.) Whichever means brings results, always do your homework on the organizations and – most importantly – the schools that you find. There are some great teachers of Taekwondo but, like any specialist activity, just as there are some who are very good, there are, equally, those who are not so good at passing on the technical skills they have personally acquired. In your enthusiasm to sign up, therefore, do not be tempted to opt for the first one you find.

CLASSES FOR CHILDREN

If you are looking on behalf of a child, you need to be sure that the classes are structured especially for children. It would be inappropriate to expect a child to learn in an adult class for many reasons. Children have lower attention spans and therefore need to be taught differently. They respond positively to lots of encouragement and praise and, though discipline is vital in Taekwondo, it can be mixed in subtly to provide a fun-filled atmosphere for youngsters to enjoy their training.

THINGS TO CONSIDER

If you are seeking to learn yourself, and you are mature enough to make your own choices without guidance from a parent or guardian, you should try to visit as many dojangs as you can before making your decision. Of course, the location and training times are an important consideration, as these must fit in with your lifestyle and existing responsibilities, but take time to observe the class and the behaviour of those in it. Don't be influenced by flamboyant surroundings, as this is not necessarily an indication of good tuition.

Upon your arrival, identify the principal instructor and introduce yourself. Explain your interest in Taekwondo and ask if it is acceptable to observe a class in session before committing yourself to the unknown. Taekwondo has nothing to hide and should not be secretive or shrouded in mystery, so (although it is highly unlikely) if your request is refused, leave immediately and continue looking elsewhere.

The Master/instructor will help you to feel relaxed and welcome, as he or she will be aware that you are stepping into a new environment that can perhaps seem strange to the outsider. At this stage, you will want to know what is involved in taking up the study of Taekwondo, and what you can expect from your early experiences. Listen carefully to what the Master tells you, as so many beginners often have unrealistic expectations of what they will be able to do after their first few weeks.

You may have many questions and there may not be time to deal with them all on this occasion, but you are entitled to know what is expected of you and (in return) what you should expect from Taekwondo. You should not sign up to the unknown, and there will inevitably be a number of essential points that you will want to get answers to, so a list of appropriate questions to ask as a prospective newcomer has been compiled in the box opposite, as a guide.

QUESTIONS TO ASK

Here's a list of useful questions to ask when you visit a dojang:

- Which classes would be appropriate for you?
- How often are you expected to attend?
- What are the associated costs to you – in particular, the joining fees and training costs?
- What should you know before taking part in your first lesson?
- What should you wear?

Check that the class sizes are not too large and make sure that everyone can see the instructor. Notice the focus of the training sessions: is the emphasis on competition work (sparring practice), stamina training or a good mix of many aspects of Taekwondo?

Try to speak to other students at the club, as they can share some of the experiences they have had since beginning their training. This will give you valuable insight into the school and will help you to decide on your final choice. Remember that it is your choice alone that is important. You may decide, for instance, that you want to practise on more occasions than is possible at this club, so you might also want to ask if it is acceptable for you to practise at other dojangs, to supplement your studies.

PRACTICAL CONSIDERATIONS

You should understand that Taekwondo is a very effective system of self-defence and, in uncontrolled hands, can be dangerous. With any such activity there are always associated risks inherent in the practice, so you need to establish with the principal instructor what level of insurance policy exists for the practitioners, and whether any supplementary policy is required. If the group is registered with the National Governing Body for sport, then this should all be taken care of in your joining fee.

Finally, make sure that you are comfortable with the type of training offered, and that you have a good feeling about the standards and behaviour of the students being taught. Good luck in your quest. Your journey has begun.

In the dojang. Grand Master PARK Soo Nam, of the World Taekwondo Federation, guides the class as they perform poomsae Keumgang *for Black Belts.*

Dojang discipline and conduct

Self-discipline is fundamental to the principles of Taekwondo. Equally, respect and good behaviour are essential to the classroom environment of the dojang. Without these values, Taekwondo would be regarded by many as little more than organized fighting. In the wrong hands Taekwondo can be a dangerous weapon, capable of inflicting grave harm on its victim. The Taekwondo Master is considered a responsible leader within the community, and takes his or her duty seriously. The Master's dojang will therefore be a place of order and calm, where you will be able to focus on your practice exclusively and without distractions.

From very early on in your training, you will be introduced to the rules of conduct to which you will be expected to conform. These may be written in your enrolment notes, posted up on the wall, or perhaps passed from senior to junior. Whichever method is employed, you should make every effort to learn the rules and adopt them into your training regime from the outset. Though they may vary slightly according to the teaching style of the Master, and from region to region, they will follow the basic and essential beliefs worthy of the tradition of Taekwondo. A list of common rules is set out below, to give you an idea of what to expect.

RULES OF CONDUCT

As a guide, you should embrace the following conventions:

- *Always bow upon entering and leaving the dojang, as well as to your instructor or partner before receiving instruction.*

- *Always arrive in time to begin class, but if you should arrive late wait to be invited by the instructor to join the group.*

- *Be polite and courteous at all times, speaking in a calm and thoughtful manner.*

- *Keep your dobok (uniform) clean and presentable at all times.*

- *Place your outdoor shoes in the designated area.*

- *Do not speak when the instructor is speaking.*

- *Never drag your belt across the floor or discard it while changing into or out of uniform.*

- *Do not smoke or consume alcohol at any time while in uniform.*

- *Do not chew gum or use offensive language in the dojang.*

- *Respect all members, particularly your seniors.*

- *Do not take advantage of juniors when practising together.*

- *Never use Taekwondo outside of the dojang unless in self-defence or in defence of the weak, and then only use the minimum force necessary.*

- *Do not brag or boast of your Taekwondo abilities.*

- *Remember the first rule of self-defence: avoid conflict whenever possible.*

The bow

The standing bow (*kyung ye*) demonstrates many things in Taekwondo. It is a show of mutual respect and confidence when exchanged with your training partner both before and after working together. It is also a mark of courtesy and humility when performed toward your instructor (*sabumnim*) at the start and end of a period of instruction. And it is an expression of loyalty and honour when entering and leaving the dojang. It should be performed slowly (to a four-second count) and with sincerity in every case.

1 Begin by standing in the upright position, feet together, and the thumbs of your closed hands pointing down the outside seam of your trousers. This is known as attention stance (*charyeot seogi*).

2 Keeping your legs and arms straight, bend forward at the waist roughly 20 degrees (or a little more). Look downwards while tilting your head further to approximately 70–90 degrees.

*FRONT VIEW

Hints and tips

- Do not try to look at your partner while bowing, as this implies mistrust and doubt. If you think that an opponent is going to attack you while you are looking down, then don't be foolish enough to bow. Remember: this is not a symbolic gesture performed outside the dojang in a real self-defence situation.

Dojang discipline and conduct *continued*

WHAT TO WEAR

Having decided to join the classes, you now need to know what is acceptable attire for your first few lessons. It would be unreasonable to expect you to purchase special clothing from the outset, so check with the instructor for local preferences according to customs in your part of the world. It needs to be something loose and unrestricting, as you are going to be sitting on the floor, stretching in all directions and kicking/swinging your legs up high. In my classes, new students are advised to wear a plain T-shirt with tracksuit trousers or jogging pants.

As Taekwondo is practised bare-foot, you should also ensure that your feet (and hands) are clean and your fingernails and toenails clipped short. This is to reduce the chances of spreading infection should an accident occur and you break the skin of your training partner.

For safety reasons you must remove all sharp objects, such as coins in pockets and items of jewellery, including studs, necklaces and rings. If a ring cannot be removed, wrap a strip of tape round your finger to cover it. Whatever you wear, be careful to ensure that you have no metal belt buckles or large zips that might also cause injury to yourself or another. If you have to wear glasses during class, make sure they are of the safety type that will not break into sharp pieces if accidentally dislodged during practice.

BASIC RULES TO REMEMBER

- Wash hands and feet before class
- Keep fingernails and toenails clipped short
- Wear loose clothing
- Empty your pockets
- Remove any sharp objects and tape up rings
- Practise tying the belt
- Turn around before adjusting your uniform
- Bow before rejoining class activity

Remember that you will be exercising and perspiring during training, so for your own health and well-being don't forget to bring some outdoor clothing to change into after showering at the end of class.

OBTAINING YOUR UNIFORM

After a few weeks you may wish to obtain a proper Taekwondo uniform (*dobok*). This will help you to feel more a part of the group, and you may actually find that you perform better as a result. Visit your local sportswear stores, or enquire with your instructor, who may have negotiated special purchase rates from suppliers for their club members. Prices vary according to quality, supplier and region, so it would not be appropriate here to give a guide to what you should expect to pay. Consider also that you might be able to obtain a bargain from the club secretary if someone has outgrown their own uniform, or from a past member of the club.

HOW TO WEAR YOUR DOBOK

When you receive your own dobok, ask one of the senior members to show you the correct way to wear it, as it is not like other clothing. Take time to learn how to fix your belt properly, as it is very long and easy to tie incorrectly (step-by step instructions on how to tie the belt are given opposite). Wear the uniform with pride, keeping it clean and always well pressed, and take every opportunity during class to make adjustments to it so that it remains looking presentable throughout. Before adjusting your clothing or re-fixing the belt, it is a custom in Taekwondo always to turn your back to your partner or instructor, but don't forget to bow when you turn back again before continuing with your training. Remember: an untidy student is usually accompanied by a sloppy attitude towards training.

Tying the belt

This procedure can be a little awkward in the beginning and many students look for an alternative, easier way of securing the belt. This usually results in the belt being crossed at the back, which not only looks very untidy but is also quite wrong. After a little practice this method will become quite easy to perform, so stick with it.

1 Hold one end in front of the navel using the fingers of the left hand, allowing sufficient length of the free end to hang down in front. Collect the rest in your right hand, ready to pay out as you pass it clockwise around your waist.

2 Now feed the portion of belt in your right hand around your waist until you reach the same position with your hands as in Step 1. You now have two layers of belt held at the navel.

3 Repeat Step 2 to give you three layers of the belt held at the navel between the fingers and thumb of the left hand.

4 Now pass the portion remaining in your right hand underneath and up behind all layers of the belt. This will ensure that the layers are held neatly together during your training session.

5 Pull the belt tight according to your required comfort, and adjust the two ends so that they are of equal length when compared to one another.

6 Now take the end you are holding in your right hand (the end you have just passed behind the three belt layers) and fold it over the top of the other end, feeding it through the centre gap that is formed.

7 Simply pull the knot that you have made and the belt is now finished. All that remains is to check, to make sure that both lengths are still equal when hanging from the knot.

Hints and tips

- Don't let your belt drag on the floor when tying it. It represents all your hard work and should be worn with pride, so don't let it get dirty as it won't take well to being washed. If it becomes untied or loose during training, bow to excuse yourself from the class, turn your back to your instructor and fellow students, and make your adjustments.

The grading system

The grading system has been devised as a series of formal tests to measure the student's ability and skill in Taekwondo. Your association will have a published syllabus for each level, which may vary slightly from one country to another, but will always follow a general theme that ensures students of the same rank are equally competent.

RANK STRUCTURE

You will enter the rank structure at White Belt level, or 10th grade (10th Keup). This belt indicates that the wearer is just beginning in Taekwondo and, after a period of approximately two to three months, and depending on the number of hours of training

10TH KEUP

9TH KEUP

8TH KEUP

BLACK BELT

POOM GRADE
(JUNIOR/UNDER-16)

7TH KEUP

1ST KEUP

6TH KEUP

2ND KEUP

5TH KEUP

3RD KEUP

4TH KEUP

received, you will be able to apply to present yourself for promotion to the next level (9th Keup). This grade is indicated by the presence of a yellow bar (the colour of the next-grade belt) around each end of the white belt. A word of caution: many students, particularly the younger ones, are often too impatient when it comes to gradings and tend to want to climb the promotional ladder far too quickly. Listen to, and follow, the advice given by your instructor in this regard, as it is far better to be a good Yellow Belt than a poor Green Belt. Different people learn at different speeds, and there is no sense in trying to compete with others in the class to get to the next grade first. Don't forget, of course, that the disappointment associated with failure is far worse than the few weeks of waiting if you are not quite ready.

GRADING TESTS

As a general rule, for the first grading test you will have to show to your examiners that you have a basic understanding of Taekwondo. You will be expected to perform the first in the series of *poomsae* ('patterns', or 'forms' – more on these later in the book), as well as demonstrate some simple attacking and defending movements with good posture, and using the correct hand or foot shape for the strike or block, and so on.

As you advance through the colours towards the Red Belt, the grading test becomes progressively more complex. Here the senior students will be expected to perform combinations of the more advanced techniques involving jumping or flying kicks, more sophisticated poomsae, sparring with one or several partners and, in the case of adults, possibly breaking techniques (also known as *kyukpa*). These involve smashing wooden boards or other material, such as roof tiles, building bricks, cement blocks or concrete slabs, the purpose of which is to demonstrate – among other things – one's power and concentration when applying Taekwondo technique. This is a daunting prospect that the beginner need not be concerned with, as it is still some way off (more about breaking later, on pages 136–7).

EARNING YOUR BLACK BELT

When you have been promoted to 1st Keup (red belt with black bars) you will have been practising for upwards of two years, and will now be focused on earning the much-coveted Black Belt. This is a deciding point in your Taekwondo career, as you will have toiled long and hard, perfecting your technical abilities in preparation for this important step. If you are successful, you will become qualified to the rank of 1st Dan. Your gradings will now be spaced further apart and your training will take on a new dimension as you learn different skills that may include specialist activities such as competition refereeing, instructing others and first aid training.

No matter how long it takes, you will feel a great sense of achievement when you are rewarded with your next grade. Take good care of your belt and wear it with pride.

GRADES AND BELT COLOURS

• 10TH KEUP	white belt	
• 9TH KEUP	white belt, yellow bars	
• 8TH KEUP	yellow belt	
• 7TH KEUP	yellow belt, green bars	
• 6TH KEUP	green belt	
• 5TH KEUP	green belt, blue bars	
• 4TH KEUP	blue belt	
• 3RD KEUP	blue belt, red bars	
• 2ND KEUP	red belt	
• 1ST KEUP	red belt, black bars	
• POOM GRADE	red/black striped belt	
• BLACK BELT		

About this book

So, now you have decided to take up the study of Taekwondo. Having read the preceding pages you now know a little more about the art, where it comes from, what to look for when choosing a suitable dojang, what to wear for your first lessons, how to conduct yourself in class, what to expect from your early experiences and how the grading and promotion system works. You have everything you need to 'make the grade', right? Well, not quite.

DEDICATION

Unless you can afford to receive personal one-to-one tuition from the Master – and, let's face it, that's not going to be many of us – you are going to be stepping into a class of maybe ten, twenty or even as many as thirty other students of varying degrees of ability and experience. If you are fortunate, you may be in a class consisting of beginners only, perhaps following a recruitment campaign. This is good, as you will all be starting from the same base level and the classes will therefore be structured towards the novice. However, even if you join a class with several different grades of students, this has clear advantages too, as you will be practising alongside the more senior grades and will be able to observe and learn from their example.

Either way, you should not be under any illusions about how easy you will find Taekwondo training. By definition, Taekwondo is an art, and that means that it requires skill in order to perform it properly. To acquire this skill takes more than just repetition and practice of the physical movements. It also requires knowledge and understanding, and this is where this book comes in.

USING THIS BOOK IN YOUR TRAINING

A well-structured lesson from a true Taekwondo Master will be informative as well as demanding in many ways. You will inevitably have lots of questions arising from your instruction that you may potentially feel awkward asking in front of others, or during class. Many instructors encourage questions, as this inevitably promotes comprehension. He or she will be patient and sympathetic with your queries, but you should avoid interrupting the flow of the training session too many times, as this interferes with the concentration of others within the group. This book is an ideal supplement to your training, and provides a handy reference guide to some of the finer details that will assist you in getting the best from your tuition – and ultimately raising your standard. You can use it in the privacy of your own home to gain a deeper appreciation of the application of each of the techniques that you will be learning. The instructions for each of the basic techniques are broken down into easy-to-follow steps, and if you pay particular attention to the *Hints and tips* boxes included throughout, these will help you to develop outstanding technique.

You will find it a valuable aid to that which you are learning in the dojang, particularly if you are not able to attend classes as often as you would like. The book covers all of the areas you are likely to experience in your first years of training, from the importance of thorough warm-ups to the complex self-defence techniques (*hosinsul*) used by advanced students, and from the basics of blocking and striking to the superior techniques employed in breaking. It's all here.

GETTING THE MOST FROM IT

Study it well, and try hard to employ the principles contained within. My purpose in writing this book is not to replace the most important factor in your learning process, for that is always going to be your instructor. My principal objective is to complement your training by helping you to acquire exceptional technique. I do not promise that it will be easy, and anyone in Taekwondo who tries to tell you that it is is merely attempting to fool you. By sharing my insight with you, gained through an exciting and successful career spanning four decades, I hope to give a little more back to the sport and martial art that has been so good to me. My sincere wish is that you will find this book as rewarding to read as I have found it to write.

The team

You are all set to begin your training. In the following pages you are going to be shown not just the basics of Taekwondo, but also what I consider to be some essential tips – gained from over thirty years' training – that will ensure you get off to a really good start. The techniques I have selected give you a balanced and comprehensive foundation in this truly unique martial art.

My team of assistants has been carefully chosen from among the very best in their respective fields to help illustrate the range of techniques covered here. I am sure that you will find their contribution helpful in your training.

On the left is Hayley Hudson. By the age of twenty she became the first ever European Technical Champion from the United Kingdom, as well as holding the accolade of eight-times undefeated National Champion of Great Britain.

Next, on my left, is Paul Green. Paul is without doubt one of the foremost

Taekwondo talents in the world today. A member of the Great Britain National Kyurugi Team, by the age of twenty-five Paul was known and feared worldwide, having won Gold medals in most Open International competitions in recent years throughout the European continent. Paul graduated in 1996 from a highly successful career in the National Junior Team, and has since defeated several World Champions as a Senior Fin Weight.

On the right is Charlene Mongelard, also a member of the Great Britain National Kyurugi Team. By the age of nineteen, Charlene had been a successful competitor at both Junior and Senior divisions, winning a host of medals for her country, and now trains full-time in Taekwondo in her quest for Olympic Gold.

Whether you are a complete beginner, or a budding Black Belt in the making, I hope that you will be inspired by the illustrated Taekwondo instruction that now follows.

Part two
Training

You are now ready to begin your training. This section features step-by-step instructions for the basic stances, punches, blocks, strikes and kicks that will become the foundations of your Taekwondo practice. Selected poomsae (patterns) are also included, for practice on your journey toward your Black Belt. And the importance of proper and thorough stretching is highlighted, as well as the principles of correct movement, which will have a direct influence on the quality of your techniques throughout your training. Take time to learn these essentials, and try to temper any haste you may have to flick through to the sections on advanced techniques.

We also look at expectations: yours, which should be sensible, and those of the Master, when you join the dojang as a new student. It is important to recognize that both must be realistic if you are to be rewarded with successes from an early stage. You won't become a Master overnight, so keep your feet on the ground and set your short-term goals within reach.

Your Taekwondo training

Now that you have got this far, having found a dojang with a good instructor, it is time for the most important question: *How long will it be before you get your Black Belt?*

It's a reasonable question that has been asked by thousands of people before you, and the answer is the same the world over. If this is your aim – and it should be – then you need to consider a few principles about Taekwondo. First, you should acknowledge that you are embarking on a journey; it is going to be a long road to reach your goal, and there will be few short cuts along the way. Just how long it will take is largely down to the factors discussed below.

YOUR AGE

While it is a fact that Taekwondo can be enjoyed by everyone – from five years old to well into one's senior years – the younger you are when you begin, the more energy you have and so the quicker you will develop the technical competences that will get you through those early grading tests to earn your belts. So, although it is entirely realistic to expect that you will enhance your life through Taekwondo, if you have aspirations to be the best, or to participate in the Olympic Games, then you will need to start young.

YOUR ATTITUDE AND MOTIVATION

Merely joining a school and taking part in the classes may not be sufficient to realize your dreams. Make no mistake, Taekwondo is hard and requires considerable effort, but it is also extremely enjoyable and immensely rewarding. Due to its popularity, there are exceptionally high numbers of people who take up the martial art and then quit soon after because they realize that they have to work hard in order to achieve the levels of superior ability that they observe in the advanced students. As a young boy having a particularly bad day in class many years ago, my instructor saw that I was not applying myself as well as usual and told me, 'Nothing is for nothing', meaning that I could not expect to get anything out of my Taekwondo if I did not put anything into it. I have never forgotten that simple phrase as it fits so well – not just in the practice of Taekwondo, but in life in general.

YOUR NATURAL ABILITY

Some people have a gift for music. There are those who can pick up virtually any musical instrument and, after a short time, produce sounds that would

seem to suggest that they are no stranger to it. There are others who have a gift for numbers, and seem to be able to arrive almost instantly at answers for complex mathematical problems that you and I would need the help of a calculator to compute. The same is also true for physical activities, and I have had the pleasure of teaching students who have shown a natural talent for Taekwondo almost from the very first lesson. If you are naturally flexible with your limbs, you will find it far easier than someone who has to struggle even to touch their toes.

This is not to say, however, that natural flexibility is a prerequisite for learning Taekwondo and going on to be good at it. I have conversely welcomed the exact opposite kind of beginner into my classes – someone with no obvious flair and very little coordination. All possess potential. I firmly believe that it is within all of us to succeed, if only we discover which keys to press to bring out the latent capacity. The more natural ability you have, the easier you will adapt to the demands of practising Taekwondo; the less you have, that little bit harder you'll have to work. To be honest, I prefer the student who works hard, because in my experience these are the ones who value what they achieve far more than those who do not have to apply themselves.

YOUR ABILITY TO PRACTISE

For the average person to be exceptional at anything requires hard work and regular practice. If your lifestyle only permits you to train once per week, you are going to have to adjust your expectations accordingly. Miss a session through illness or an unexpected domestic situation, and it will be two weeks between classes. This will slow down your progress, as you will need to spend more time refreshing yourself with what you learned on the previous occasion. Those who are able to attend classes twice or more per week are clearly going to see quicker improvements in stamina, technical ability and general comprehension, over a sustained period. Today's world moves ever faster, and we often have less time than we would like for new pursuits. If this sounds familiar, don't be downbeat – just modify your outlook to be more realistic in terms of how long it is going to take to achieve your goals.

YOUR INSTRUCTOR

Of course, without any of the above, your ability to excel is going to be that much more difficult, but one further aspect should not be overlooked.

Your Taekwondo training *continued*

You cannot do it alone, nor with any one book – even this one. As mentioned earlier, you are going to need the help and guidance of a qualified and experienced instructor. This needs to be someone with a sincere wish to help *you* achieve your potential, for that is their role in the process.

Like any sport, business or profession, there are genuine experts in their respective fields but there are also the fraudsters, and it would be wrong to suggest that Taekwondo is immune to such imitators. My advice is beware the instructor who uses overbearing discipline, or any kind of chastisement in the class. Similarly, you should avoid those who demand excessively high tuition charges to support grandiose lifestyles. These people are unlikely to have learned true Taekwondo and are often more interested in performing for their own gratification rather than from a genuine desire to pass on their knowledge and expertise to you. A good instructor is one who is interested in helping you to achieve your ambition and your desires through the pursuit of Taekwondo.

TYPICAL LESSON FORMAT

Different dojangs will have their own systems based on the emphasis placed on the various elements of Taekwondo training that the instructor wishes to focus on, but all will generally follow a logical sequence from beginning to end.

A typical lesson will include a formal line-up of the students before beginning the warm-up exercises that will prepare each member for the more rigorous regime to follow. The class will form straight lines facing the instructor, with the most senior member to the front and on the right. Members will then assemble in ranks beside and behind in order of grade, with the newest members at the back and to the left. This might seem a little odd to the novice, but it is a very effective way of allowing beginners to learn from the senior members by observing their actions and copying while being instructed.

WARM-UP AND BASICS

Class will begin with the most senior member calling the group to come to attention, followed by the command to bow to the instructor. This gesture will be returned and followed by a period of warming-up exercises (a more detailed explanation of which can be found overleaf). Practise with diligence during this important stage of preparation, as this will be followed by a segment of more strenuous stretching exercises to improve your capacity to perform the high kicking techniques that Taekwondo is so renowned for.

When the class is fully warmed up and stretched out it will be time to practise and develop the fundamental techniques of Taekwondo, such as blocking, striking, kicking, stepping and jumping, before moving on to the potentially more hazardous aspects such as sparring and self-defence work. These basics are the cornerstone of your Taekwondo capability on which all other elements will depend for success. Again, my message to you is to practise hard to condition your body, mind and spirit to become strong, sharp and focused. It is also essential during this process that you comprehend the essence of what you are doing, as these are not simply theoretical movements dependent on your imagination for success – quite the opposite, in fact. They are proven attack and defence actions that, when performed correctly, are exceptionally powerful, fast and, therefore, effective in the combat situation. Be absolutely certain that you understand what you are meant to be trying to achieve, and precisely how you are supposed to perform each of the skills in turn. If it is not clear to you in class and it is permitted to ask questions during training, then do so, as it will be far easier once you know the objectives of these otherwise alien moves.

PARTNER WORK

After you have understood and rehearsed several attacking and defensive applications against imaginary opponents, you may be split into pairs for practice with a partner. Strict control and discipline must be observed during this stage, as this is where the potential for accidents and consequent injuries is highest. No one should expect to inflict or receive damage during training, and pain is not conducive to learning, so remember and observe the principal precept of mutual respect that is reinforced by the bow, which precedes and follows this part of the lesson. Treat your partner with the same reverence that you expect from them – you will learn quicker.

Sparring takes several forms. For the novice there are pre-arranged attack-and-defence sequences that are designed to familiarize the practitioner with a variety of differing responses in given situations. These sequences range from three-step movements – whereby the defender has the opportunity to practise three blocks against similar attacks before counter-striking – to one-step movements offering less opportunity before the defender is expected to perform an appropriate response.

Another form of sparring involves semi-free style interaction, where the two participants alternately attack one another with fast-flowing and varied kicking techniques. This provides each participant with the opportunity to develop rhythm and timing as well as coordination and reflex action. All of the above sparring types are essential preparation for the free-sparring performed by the more advanced students in the class, or competition fighting performed at domestic- or international-level tournaments.

ADVANCED TECHNIQUES
Self-defence training is usually reserved for advanced students later in the class, and involves close-up attacks that require the defender to release from holds, grapples or attacks with weapons. Here the objectives are to disarm, apply pressure to joints or throw the attacker to the floor before delivering a final and decisive strike. This provides the opportunity to practise and improve a range of counter-measures against an assailant that are considered inappropriate to other types of sparring practice. The ability to fall safely in the event of

being thrown to the ground is essential, and required learning in order to avoid injury to oneself.

For advanced students over junior level, there exists one further component to the typical class, and this is commonly known as 'breaking' or 'destruction'. Here the student is given the chance to test the power and accuracy of the techniques learned, by applying them to sections of boards (timber). To the beginner it appears that the sole purpose is merely to smash the target object. Although this is a very satisfying part of training, as it gives the student positive and immediate feedback as to their technical ability, it exists for more than simple self-gratification. It is a test of mental as well as physical conditioning. It reinforces correct application, underlines the significance of acceleration through the technique and focuses concentration on the task at hand. Interestingly, when the time comes for you to experience this aspect of your Taekwondo, you will no doubt have to relearn many of your previously most-trusted techniques.

THE WARM-DOWN
The final stage of the lesson will be given to the warm-down exercises. This will take a similar form to the start of class, as it is equally important that you take time to return your body smoothly to a normal state of equilibrium following the arduous and demanding activity of the last hour or two. Warm-downs are a series of callisthenics that gently stretch the muscles you have just worked while your heart rate is returned to normal, thus reducing the chances of discomfort and soreness that may be felt the following morning, caused as a direct result of strenuous exercise.

Each part of the lesson has unique significance and should not be thought of as any less important than the next. Apply yourself with total commitment to improvement with each and every repetition of a given motion. Performed with such sincerity and diligence, your progress will be faster, your training more satisfying and your rewards more plentiful.

Warming up

The following pages introduce the first – and arguably the most important – element in your training regime: the warm-up routine.

THE IMPORTANCE OF THE WARM-UP

It is essential that you take due care and time over this aspect of your training, as improper or insufficient preparation is one of the major causes of potential injury to the martial artist. The very nature of Taekwondo movements requires the body's muscles, tendons, joints and ligaments to be warm and supple if they are to be expected to respond to the demands of intensive and repetitive exertion. For ultimate success, all of the actions involved in Taekwondo depend on fast responses either to the spoken command of an instructor or to offensive movements from an opponent or partner. Your body therefore needs to be appropriately conditioned and prepared to be able to deliver this type of explosive performance.

Your warm-up routine also serves another purpose besides that mentioned above, for when you prepare in this way several changes take place inside the body, with the release of naturally produced chemicals into the bloodstream that enhance performance and heighten both concentration and awareness. All this adds up to a more efficient and effective training experience, which you will agree is always desirable.

▲ CAUTION

- *Some warm-up exercises are not suitable for young children – check with your instructor first.*
- *Discuss any injuries or medical conditions with your instructor before attempting any exercises; he or she will advise you on what will be appropriate in your circumstances.*

LENGTH OF WARM-UP

Different climates and seasons affect the time that you will need to spend warming up. If it is very warm outside you may only need to spend ten to twenty minutes limbering up and stretching. However, if it is cold you may need to more than double the time spent, to ensure that you are thoroughly prepared for what comes after. Another factor is the time of day you choose to practise. A morning session will require you to pay more attention to stretching than an evening session, when your body has been active through the day. You must be the final judge – but whatever you decide don't cheat yourself, or sooner or later you will pay a heavy price.

YOUR WARM-UP ROUTINE

Begin your routine by loosening off the joints – ankles, knees, hips, shoulders, elbows and wrists – gently

shaking them out and rotating them through their full range of movement. Follow this with some gentle jogging for several minutes to raise your heartbeat and pulse rate. When you begin to feel warm and start to show signs of perspiring, you may begin some of the more gentle stretching exercises shown on the following pages. It should be remembered that some of the exercises in general use are not always suitable for young children, whose bones are still growing and who may suffer from stretched ligaments as a result of their muscles being less able to resist the effects of certain exercises. (This is another good reason for separate classes for adults and juniors.) Your instructor will guide you in terms of what may or may not be appropriate, but do remember to discuss any injuries or medical conditions you may have that might be adversely affected by any form of exercise.

The routine I have outlined will bring you to the point where you can begin your Taekwondo training, but (if your lesson permits) don't leave it there. I would advise further stretching during your various stages of practice, to improve and develop your flexibility for the high kicking Taekwondo is so well-known for.

WARMING DOWN

When your class or training session is nearing the end, it is wise to go through a final series of more gentle 'warming-down' exercises, to return your body to its normal state after intensive exertion.

WARM-UP CHECKLIST

Never try to skip a warm-up for any reason – time-related or otherwise. Always keep in mind the main reasons for warming-up:

- It's vital for the muscles, tendons, joints and ligaments to be warm and supple, to avoid injury.
- A conditioned body means your responses will be quicker and your techniques more effective.
- The chemical reaction within the body during a warm-up enhances performance and heightens concentration.

By spending five to ten minutes this way, you will gently stretch out the muscle groups that have been working hard during training, and this will go a long way towards improving your permanent flexibility and also warding off the chances of aches and soreness that beginners often complain of in the days following a hard work-out.

Warm-ups • *Arm swings*

This exercise is designed to mobilize your shoulders and waist. It is also very useful for improving your coordination skills. This is a very safe routine, so you can practise quite vigorously as long as you have sufficient room.

Hints and tips

• Keep the hips turning during the two-way swing and gradually build a little more speed in the swing as you progress. Though it sounds easy, many people get confused and lose rhythm almost immediately. Stick with it – you can even have fun trying it out with family or friends.

✱ BACKWARDS

1 Begin by standing upright with your feet roughly shoulder-width apart. Hold your arms straight up above your head, keeping your hands open and your back straight throughout the movement. Now, rotate both arms slowly in a forward direction eight to ten times, gradually increasing the speed of the swing. Repeat this in a backward direction.

2 Now for the difficult bit. From the start position, begin swinging the left arm slowly in a backward direction. As soon as you can, increase the arc of the swing by twisting your waist to the left side. Now, without interrupting your movement, begin swinging your right arm in the opposite direction. Do eight to ten rotations, before repeating in the opposite direction.

Warm-ups • *Waist twists*

This exercise is good for improving upper-body mobility (shoulders, chest, upper and lower back, waist, plus hips and knees). Imagine you are pivoting on a vertical axis through the centre of your body.

1 Stand with your feet approximately shoulder-width apart and hold your arms out straight in front of your shoulders.

2 Keeping your feet still, rotate the entire body to the left, looking as far round as you can. Keep your hands level with your shoulders throughout and feel the stretching action all the way down through your body.

3 Return to the centre and repeat the twist to the other side. Continue twisting in a fluid motion from one side to the other, until you have completed between eight and ten full twists.

> ▲ CAUTION
>
> • *Keep your torso straight and your spine vertical throughout the twisting action, otherwise you will place undue strain on your muscles.*

Warm-ups • *Side bends*

This exercise is good for your side, hook and turning kicks, as it improves the agility of your waist and hips. Remember to lean to the opposite side of the extended arm, and keep the arm straight throughout.

▲ CAUTION
• *As with all exercise, work to your limitations. If you feel any pain, ease back immediately. Forget the old adage of 'no pain, no gain' – this is a major cause of injury.*

1 Again, stand with your feet roughly shoulder-width apart for stability, but this time with your right arm held straight up above your head and your left hand resting on your hip.

2 Without leaning forward, bend as far as you can to the left, keeping your raised arm straight and close to your head for that little bit more of a stretch. Return to the centre and repeat to the opposite side. Do three or four repetitions on both sides, holding each stretch for a count of ten.

Warm-ups • *Back bends*

This exercise is for your back, pelvis and thighs, and should be done slowly to maintain balance. Don't worry about how far you are able to bend to begin with – you should find your suppleness increasing with practice. If you find that you over-balance, step out a little wider with your feet.

▲ CAUTION
• *Don't try this exercise if you have any kind of back complaint, as you could make the condition worse.*

This time, stand with your feet about one-and-a-half to two times shoulder-width apart, and place your hands on your hips. Bend your knees and, keeping your feet firmly on the floor, bend backwards as far as you can comfortably manage. Hold for a count of five to ten, and repeat four to five times.

Hints and tips

• Try to fix your eyes on something immovable so that if you wobble at all you can come back up before losing your balance completely.

Warm-ups • *Crunches*

This routine exercises and strengthens your stomach and abdomen, while at the same time improving your sense of balance – vital in Taekwondo practice. Two different methods cater for differing levels of ability.

> ▲ CAUTION
>
> • *Don't try to do old-style sit-ups (locking your fingers behind your head), as this can seriously damage your neck.*

Hints and tips

• Keep your knees and feet together and try to look straight ahead, concentrating on maintaining your balance throughout the movements.

METHOD 1

1 Lie down on your back on the floor and raise your heels up a little, placing your hands on your thighs. To ease the pressure on your lower back, bend your knees very slightly.

2 Now draw your knees up to your chest while sliding your hands forward along the line of your legs as you sit up. Return to the start position and only rest your heels down if you are having difficulty. Repeat five to ten times.

METHOD 2

1 As an alternative for the stronger learner, adopt the same start position but this time hold onto your earlobes. This increases the tension in the stomach, and places more weight on the upper body.

2 Just as before, sit up and draw your knees to your chest, but make sure you don't pull on your ears for reasons that will become obvious if you try it! Repeat ten to twenty times.

Warm-ups • *Pikes*

This exercise works in a similar way to crunches, but takes your skills of balance up a notch. Don't worry if you find that you topple backwards the first few times you try it, as you'll soon begin to feel the point of balance with practice.

Hints and tips

• Again, keep your knees, feet and hands together during this movement. You will improve your balance very quickly if you follow these routines.

1 Again, lie down on your back, but this time with your arms outstretched behind your head. As before, don't lock your knees, and raise your heels up a little off the floor.

2 Point your toes and sit up, bringing your arms over your head and raising your feet up to meet your hands in front of you, keeping your arms and legs straight throughout. Lower gently to the start position and repeat five times, increasing with your personal ability.

Stretches • *Leg swings*

These exercises are great for resetting your lower-body mobility (when you might be feeling tightness in the legs following a previous training session, for instance), and should be performed both before and after the static stretches covered in your classes. As always, it is important that good posture be maintained throughout the movements. Repeat each leg swing about ten to twelve times on each side.

1 Begin by standing with your feet shoulder-width apart and your hands held up in front of your body. You are going to use your own energy (and considerable effort) to raise each leg swiftly to its highest position, without swinging it back beyond the supporting foot first.

2 Bring your right leg up in a straight line towards your shoulder, and repeat, returning to the start position each time. Don't worry about height: your strength and flexibility will build if you concentrate on quality of technique. This swing improves your front kicks by stretching the hamstrings (back of the upper leg). Repeat with the left leg.

3 From the same start position, turn your right foot to point out to the side while keeping your body upright and facing the front. Now, using the muscles of the leg, raise it up to the side of your shoulder, as high and as briskly as you are able. Tension should again be felt in the hamstring. Repeat with the left leg.

3a If you are having difficulty maintaining your balance during this side swing, try placing your hands on something solid at waist level. (A chair or window ledge can be quite useful for all of these stretches, but make sure you are not likely to strike anything or anyone with your foot during the movement!)

4 Again, from the start position, with your feet parallel and your toes pointing towards the front, lift your right leg up to the side as high as you can, being careful not to bend forward from the waist. You will have to concentrate really hard to maintain your body alignment in order to get maximum benefit. Feel the stretch in the inner thigh. This swing is good for improving your side, turning and hook kicks. Repeat with the left leg.

5 Finally, from the start position, raise your right leg straight up to the rear, keeping its path on a line with your right hip and shoulder. Bend the knee of the swinging leg slightly but try to keep the foot pointing down throughout the movement. You can place your hands on your hips for this exercise if it feels more comfortable. This time you are stretching the front of the thigh. Repeat with the left leg.

Stretches • *Knee bends*

Although called 'knee bends' (an apt description of its action), this exercise actually works the muscles in your rump (gluteus) and the rear of the upper legs (hamstrings).

Hints and tips

- To get the most benefit from this exercise, don't lose sight of the objective – to loosen and gently stretch the hamstrings – so try hard to keep your shoulders on the same horizontal plane throughout, in order to give your muscles the maximum intended workout.

1 To begin, stand with your legs straight, your feet together and your hands on your knees, and bend forward at the waist until you feel tension in the back of the legs.

2 Now, keeping your knees together while bending them, and without raising your upper body, lower yourself into the squat position as you count 1 and 2, before returning to the previous position for the count of 3 and 4. Repeat ten to fifteen times.

Stretches • *Single-leg squats*

This is a more concentrated stretching exercise for the back of each leg in turn. In many dojangs it is commonly referred to as 'eight and eight exercise', as the lower positions are held for a count of approximately eight seconds.

Hints and tips

- Don't let yourself lean forward – a common mistake. This will cause you to lift the heel of your bending leg, resulting in a loss of balance.
- With this stretch, try to keep the knee of your bending leg in line with your shoulder for added benefit.

1 Place your feet at least double-shoulder-width apart, with your hands on your knees. Advanced students may want to try holding the ankles instead.

2 Keep your back straight and both heels on the floor while bending your left knee as much as you can. Attempt to lower your straightened leg towards the floor and hold for a count of eight. Return to the upright position and repeat on the opposite leg. Repeat four to six times with each leg.

2a This is the ultimate goal, achievable only by those with an advanced level of flexibility. Note the straightened leg on the floor, both heels down and the bent knee in line with the shoulder.

Stretches • *Seated stretches*

This is a tough exercise but has great rewards when performed regularly. It is designed to benefit your back, waist, hips and upper legs, and you can do it at home while in front of the TV – so no excuses! These positions are progressively more advanced, so don't try to push yourself beyond your capabilities too soon.

Hints and tips

- If you aren't very flexible, don't be put off. We all started like this. Avoid bending your knees to get your elbows lower in position 1; preserve the quality of your position through the stretch – don't compromise it for what you might mistakenly regard as a better result.
- Do this exercise as often as you can and you will see improvements sooner than you would imagine.

1 Sit with your legs as wide apart as you can, toes pointing up. Now, without looking down, place your hands under your chin and lean forward. Keep your back straight and try to rest your elbows on the floor. Hold your position for a count of ten to twenty, and repeat two to five times (don't bounce).

2 When you are able to touch the floor with your elbows, you are ready for this position. Reach forward with your hands as far as you can and concentrate on lowering your stomach, rather than your head, to the floor. This will be easier the wider apart your feet are, so readjust your position as you repeat the movements. Hold as Position 1.

3 Now, as you become more able, you can try this advanced move. Place a hand on each foot and turn your head to one side. You can now apply gentle assistance, with your arms acting as levers, to bring your body closer to the floor. Make sure your back remains straight throughout. Hold as Position 1.

4 For the final stretch, prepare to dip to the left by placing your left arm across your chest. Lean directly left (not forward) and reach over your head to your left foot with your right hand. Align your body by ensuring your left shoulder stays inside the left leg, not on top of it, making it easier to reach toward your foot. Hold as Position 1.

Drill

This section covers the importance of the correct body movements that are often under-emphasized or neglected in one's training. You should concentrate on your whole body when applying your techniques, rather than just the arm or leg that you are using in the action. By spending time improving *how* you arrive at the final position, you will apply your techniques more effectively and efficiently – whether you are going forwards, backwards or changing direction altogether. Try to remember that your *entire body* delivers the technique, whether it is a block or an attack. If you think of the limb as merely the tool or weapon that is being used, your techniques will be faster and stronger, and far more reliable. This will inspire confidence in your own ability, which is so vital in Taekwondo.

Hip action

First, we look at the hip action that is required to add the necessary power to your techniques, using a simple low-section block to illustrate (this is covered in more detail later – see page 54).

Hints and tips

- Spend time learning to incorporate this action into the delivery of all your techniques, initially from a standing position where you twist back and forth on the spot as you block. Try to make the free ends of your belt swing wide in an effort to increase the speed of the action.

- For a technique you can really depend on, combine all aspects of the action so that you complete the hip twist, the transfer of body weight and the block at the same moment as touching the stepping foot down into position.

WALKING STANCE

1 Turn your hips and shoulders to the side to prepare for the delivery. Always begin your step forward into walking stance by rotating your hips in this way, as this sets you up for generating the power of your block.

2 As you transfer your body weight, think about throwing your block forward using a rapid hip rotation (I call this a 'snapping' action). The knot of your belt should now be facing the front.

LONG STANCE

1 The principle is the same for long stance. Launch your move by swivelling your hips to the side as you prepare your arms.

2 Complete the block by using your hips to catapult the blocking arm to its destination.

Moving

Moving efficiently is vital to good technique. Perform these movements as quickly as possible, and without allowing the head to bob up and down. Keep the overall height constant, and try to develop a fluid action.

STEPPING

1 Begin in a left-foot-forward guarding position with the fists lightly closed and held up at shoulder level. The principle is the same whether you are launching a kick, strike or block.

2 Launch the stepping action forward by throwing the right-side hip forward as discussed on the previous page. Don't be tempted to initiate the move simply by bringing the right foot forward, as this will be too casual and slow.

SLIDING

1 The transition from defending in walking stance to counter-attacking often requires you to close the gap between your body and your opponent's. Here, you are going to slip from a middle-section block into long stance for the counter-punch (covered on pages 56 and 51).

2 Don't just slide your front leg forward as you punch. It may look simple, but when you practise this move remember to emphasize the correct action by first pulling the right-side hip back, before snapping it forward again to launch the punching fist from its start position.

SKIPPING

1 From the same start position, you are now going to skip forward to close in on your opponent.

2 Leading with the hip, bring your back foot towards your front foot and this will 'kickstart' the front foot to also move swiftly forward. By leading from the centre of your body, all other parts will move equally fast and not be a drag on your movement.

3 By skipping forward, your back foot closes in on your front foot, thus repositioning your supporting (back) foot if you are throwing a kick with the front leg. You can use these actions to attack or defend.

TURNING

1 To practise the turn, begin from a left-hand low block in long stance, and imagine that your opponent is attacking you from behind.

2 Begin your turn by pulling your hips round and pivoting clockwise on the ball of your left foot. As you do this, transfer your weight onto the left foot and bring the right foot under your body.

3 You are now set to use all of your stored power by advancing onto your right foot as you step, snapping your hip round to deliver your block.

Basic techniques

This section introduces the basic attacking and defending techniques that are directed to the three principal target areas of the opponent or training partner. These are the fundamentals that you will learn from your very first class. The following lessons contained here cover the stances, punches, blocks, strikes and kicks that will form the staples of your Taekwondo practice, from which all other forms of expression in Taekwondo will originate. Overleaf, the various hand and foot techniques that you will be using are introduced, so that you can work on getting them right before you move on to put them into practice.

LEARNING, STEP BY STEP

Step-by-step instructions are given for each technique. These allow you to better understand not just the origin, or starting position, of the moves, but also the methodology behind the delivery of each one. In this way you will be more receptive to all the significant points that will raise the performance of each of your techniques to a higher level. Pay special attention to the boxes containing the hints and tips, as these are full of valuable advice to further aid your training. The application shots (always pictured in the top-left corner) give additional help by putting the move into context, and assist you, the reader, to visualize the delivery of each action. As a further aid, directional arrows are used to indicate the path of the strike and serve to draw attention to the rotational movements of the hips, torso or legs that need to be applied in order to gain maximum effectiveness from the technique. The points of impact are also highlighted, for immediate visual understanding.

STANCES: YOUR FOUNDATIONS

The positions assumed by the body for all techniques are especially important. These postures, or stances, determine the effectiveness of the attacking or defending movements because they control the degree of balance, stability and equilibrium present in the execution of the technique. From a firm and stable base you will be more able to apply the power, speed and reactionary actions that will convert an otherwise weak and ineffective movement into a superior technique worthy of the potential Black Belt holder.

The following four basic stances are the first to be taught in Taekwondo dojangs the world over. They are walking stance (*ap seogi*), long stance (*ap koobi*), back stance (*dwit koobi*) and horse-riding stance (*joochum seogi*). Each has its own significance in a given situation, but all share one important principle: they are the foundations for proper technique, allowing the student to develop a strong and firm base from which to apply the various attacking or defending skills. Like all movements, they must be practised again and again, using different techniques and by stepping to and from different directions, until they become second nature. Experienced practitioners are expected to be able to move fluidly from one stance to another, in order to gain maximum advantage of the changing opportunities for attack and defence offered during combat situations. This skill is also further reinforced through the practice of poomsae (more about this later, on pages 90–91).

TARGET AREAS

The three target areas mentioned earlier, for both attack and defence, are known as low, middle and high sections.

LOW SECTION
Low section can actually mean any target below the horizontal line of the belt, including shin, knee, thigh, groin and the lower part of the belly, though within the training environment it is most often designated to be the groin. Attacks with the foot directed to any areas within this section include

front, turning, side and pushing kicks. Effective hand attacks directed low-section include knifehand, ridgehand and spearhand.

MIDDLE SECTION

Middle section is the general area between the belt and the shoulders. It is further defined for competition purposes as being the stomach (solar plexus) and flanks (lower ribs). All of the attacks illustrated here are appropriate to this area, but special guidelines exist concerning what are classified as acceptable and unacceptable techniques for competition purposes. Your instructor will be able to provide you with all the relevant information and rulings, should you go on to develop an interest in this type of training (see also *Note on New Competition Rules*, page 144). It is sufficient to mention here that the competition rules define the area between the back of the shoulder blades down to the base of the spine as a prohibited area, for obvious safety reasons. Any attack to this area will incur a penalty for the attacker, and could even result in forfeiture of the match if the opponent is rendered unable to continue as a result of an attack directed here. In the interests of your well-being, and that of your training partner, no further reference to this area will be made here.

HIGH SECTION

High section is the area above a horizontal line at shoulder level, but more specifically it is regarded as the face, including the side of the head, ears, neck and throat. Once again, it should be pointed out that the back of the head is disallowed in the competition environment, and so it is wise not to practise directing attacks to this area. All attacking techniques covered are suitable for use towards high-section targets.

BLOCKS

The blocking actions illustrated are the basic defence movements that prevent you from receiving a strike from your partner or opponent. Clearly, it is better

not to be in a situation where you will be struck in the first place, but if you are within range, and your opponent launches an attack in your direction, you need to be practised in deflecting the attack in order to preserve your own well-being. The blocks are directed to the same three areas of the body (high, middle and low sections) according to the target chosen by the attacker. An effective block is one made using the entire body and not just the arm. This is an important point, too frequently overlooked by the beginner. Remember that in Taekwondo it will often be your arm versus the attacker's leg, so you must practise with full commitment in order to build a reliable and trustworthy defence. As with all Taekwondo techniques, there is no substitute for practice, practice and more practice.

STRIKES AND KICKS

The strikes and kicks explained in this section have been chosen to provide you with the essential 'tools of the trade' and will need to be rehearsed many hundreds – if not thousands – of times before they may be regarded as being totally dependable. Merely raising your arm or leg into the end position is certainly not going to achieve the desired outcome. Therefore, careful consideration needs to be shown to practising the transitional movements of the body and the complementary actions of the hips and torso, as well as the reactionary movements of the opposite arm in the case of hand techniques.

IMPORTANT NOTE

As a final word, you should bear in mind that no aspect of technique explained here will work entirely effectively in isolation. You should think of all components as being parts of a whole, each movement codependent upon the other elements in order to be successful.

Hand and foot techniques

The following illustrations show the correct striking areas of both hand and foot techniques (you will soon become familiar with the area used in each technique as you progress through the book). These are the tools with which you will deliver your strike, and in time they will become extremely effective, forged into weapons by constant practice.

The importance of the ideal technique cannot be emphasized enough: it is more than simply extending the arm or leg into the final position. This may look good enough to the untrained eye, but to be truly effective it requires much more. So, before we look at how to deliver the strikes, let us take time to study the part of the hand or foot that is going to connect with the target. Spend some time making the correct shape before you then move on to reproduce it as you learn and practise the basic techniques included on the following pages.

THE FIST (*Ju mok*)

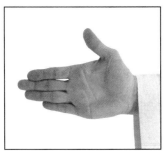

1 Begin with the hand held open, fingers together.

2 Keeping the fingers together, fold them tightly over at the secondary knuckles until the fingertips begin to touch the palm of the hand.

3 Only now should you bend the lower part of the fingers from your primary knuckles into the palm of your hand.

4 Finally, wrap your thumb across the underside of your fingers and clench firmly.

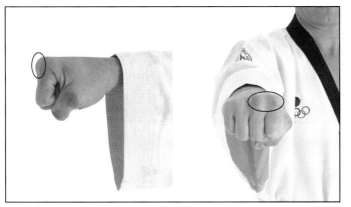

5 Don't bend your wrist. Your contact point is the front part of the knuckles of the first and second finger; by following these instructions and aligning your wrist correctly, you will be able to look along your outstretched arm to see a straight line through the forearm to the knuckles. This will allow the impact area of the forefist (*cheonkwon*) to be furthermost forward.

> ▲ **CAUTION**
>
> - *Although you want speed with the delivery of your punch (which comes from being relaxed), don't be tempted to unclench the fist during the action. Releasing the tension in the fingers will relax the muscles in your forearm, but be sure to squeeze tightly just before impact to avoid injury to your hand.*

BACKFIST
(*Deungjumeok*)

This is formed as for the forefist, but the one important difference being that the wrist is slightly bent back to ensure that the knuckles, and not the back of the hand, connect with the target.

SPEARHAND/KNIFEHAND
(*Seonkeut/Sonnal*)

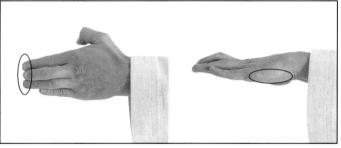

The hand shape is the same for both of these, but different contact areas are used (spearhand: fingertips / knifehand: outside edge of hand). Hold the hand out straight and pull back your thumb without allowing it to touch the fingers. Without bending at the primary knuckles, pull your middle finger back into line with the first and third fingers. Squeeze all four fingers together and keep the primary knuckles dipped low.

RIDGEHAND
(*Sonnal deung*)

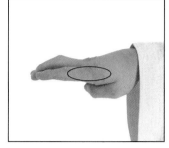

Essentially the same shape as for knifehand, but for this technique you must fold your thumb under the palm of your hand, to permit contact with the correct part of the hand (as shown here).

PALM HEEL
(*Batangson*)

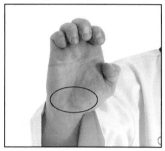

Fold your fingers at the secondary knuckles as you would in the first stage of making a fist. Bend your wrist up to 90 degrees and pull your thumb down to give added strength to the weapon. Contact is only with the base of the palm.

BALL OF FOOT
(*Ap chook*)

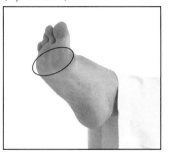

Extend your foot forward as far as you can before bending back the toes. This allows for contact with the part of the foot that you would use to depress the clutch pedal in a car. This area is used for the front kick.

FOOT SWORD
(*Balnal*)

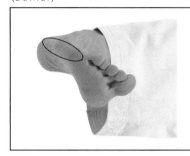

Curl your foot, including your toes, back towards your body at the same time as twisting the inside of your foot as though trying to look at the sole. This action extends the outside edge of the foot furthermost forward and is used in the side kick. The foot shape is the same for the turning kick, but instead you connect with the ball of the foot.

INSTEP
(*Baldeung*)

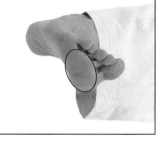

Extend the foot and toes as far forward as you can in line with your leg. This part of the foot is used for front turning kicks.

BACK OF HEEL
(*Dwitkumchi*)

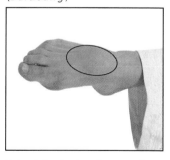

Though the contact point is clearly different, the foot shape is the same as the foot sword. This position is used for the reverse turning kick, and for hook kicks against boards.

UNDERSIDE
(*Balkeut*)

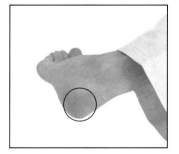

This is the same foot shape as the instep position, but this time think of connecting with the ball of your foot and underside of the extended toes. It is used for hook kicks.

BOTTOM OF HEEL
(*Dwit chook*)

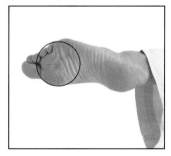

Again, this foot shape is the same as the foot sword, except here the foot points downwards and you connect with the base of the heel. This is used for the back kick.

Walking stance *Ap seogi*

This stance is an easy one for the beginner. Though we will be looking at several of the basic stances in Taekwondo, I'd like you to use this one to practise the various hand and foot techniques that are to follow. This will allow you to concentrate on each of the techniques that you are going to perform with your arms and legs without getting confused by some of the more difficult stances used in Taekwondo.

Hints and tips

- Try to stand tall in this position – don't be tempted to crouch. Remember that the most vulnerable target in Taekwondo is your head, so you want to keep it as far from your opponent's foot as possible.

FRONT VIEW
As its name implies, this stance is assumed by stepping forward as though walking naturally. Your feet should be about 30 cm (1 ft) apart, with both heels resting on the floor. Hold your body upright and turned slightly sideways to reduce the target you show to your partner or opponent.

SIDE VIEW
Your front foot should point forward, with your legs straight but the knees softened to allow for faster movements. Hold your arms up, elbows in and fists lightly closed. You are now in a guarding position, ready for action. Practise stepping back and forth, keeping your weight evenly distributed on both feet.

Long stance *Ap koobi*

This stance is very strong and gives you a feeling of confidence when used. It naturally promotes power in your techniques, and is much deeper than walking stance – hence its name. Used in conjunction with blocks and strikes, it offers better stability and purchase when developing power and speed in the formative stages of your training. It is considered a primary attacking stance, and is sometimes also referred to as 'front stance', as the weight is distributed approximately sixty per cent towards the front leg.

Hints and tips

- MY GOLDEN RULE
  Ensure that you always lock your back leg straight with your heel down to make this stance as solid as possible. To do otherwise will seriously rob your delivered technique of power.

FRONT VIEW
Step forward with your left foot, then bend your front knee until it is over your heel. Keep your back leg straight but let your rear foot turn out slightly for balance. Imagine you are walking along a set of train tracks, keeping your feet shoulder-width apart and flat to the floor, with your weight evenly distributed.

SIDE VIEW
Some of your hand techniques will require your shoulders to be turned at various degrees to the front, but always rotate your hips so that the knot of your belt is fully turned forward. This has the effect of locking your stance and giving you that feeling of added power as you thrust the technique forward.

Back stance *Dwit koobi*

This stance is shorter than long stance (by as much as half the length), and is most often used for blocking or guarding techniques. We therefore think of it as a defensive stance and tend to use it a lot in sparring practice. You will immediately notice how the body adopts a more 'side-on' position, reducing the available targets exposed to your partner.

Hints and tips

- To stop yourself tipping forward, imagine a vertical line running through the rear shoulder, hip, knee and heel.
- With your arms drawn up as shown here, you can efficiently block high, middle or low, and with either arm.

FRONT VIEW
Step back onto your right foot and turn it 90 degrees outwards, forming an 'L' shape with your feet. Now bend your back knee and transfer 60–75 per cent of your weight onto this leg by drawing your hips back. Keep your body upright and imagine that you are about to lift your front foot to kick.

SIDE VIEW
If too much weight is forward, your head will move as you shift your body weight back to kick, so try to get the feeling of 'sitting' in the stance by bending your knees a little more. Draw your arms up to shoulder height, keeping your elbows in and fists softly closed, ready to block.

Horse-riding stance   *Joochum seogi*

It is clear to see where this stance gets its name. It's a great position for developing your power when practising your blocks and strikes as it allows you to rotate equally well from either side to the finished position, since the point of balance is between the feet and the weight is equally distributed.

Hints and tips

- To help keep your back straight, imagine a vertical line running from your shoulders through your hips and down to your heels.
- Don't rise up when you perform your techniques, as this will throw off your balance and you will lose your stability.

FRONT VIEW
Place your feet about double-shoulder-width apart, with your feet pointing forward, heels down. Bend your knees out over your heels to assume the position astride your imaginary horse. Keep your back straight and your shoulders relaxed.

SIDE VIEW
As with back stance, try to stay low, 'sitting' in the stance. Practise blocking from here by turning your waist out of the position as you prepare your arms, so that you can generate the force necessary to make the block effective.

Forward punch *Baro jireugi*

The punch is the principal attack used by the upper body. Performed correctly, it has devastating power and can be applied in its various forms to many targets. A balanced and coordinated action from the opposite hand is vital (as with all hand techniques); the balance is achieved by this equal and opposite reaction to the punch, and ensures the involvement of your entire body in the attack.

Hints and tips

- Make your punch stronger and straighter by keeping your elbows in close to your body as you punch. This will be easier if you keep the fingers of the punching fist uppermost until the very end of the movement.

* SIDE VIEW

1 Prepare by drawing your hips back to the right, with your right (punching) fist on your hip, and bring your left arm up in front, ready to pull it back smartly to the hip as you deliver the punch. This coiling action ensures that you drive the punch out from your hips, thus achieving maximum power.

2 Step forward into long stance with the right foot and accelerate the punch to its target, drawing the left fist back to your hip with equal force at the same time. Here, you are punching middle section, so your target is the solar plexus. As you punch, rotate your fist so that the back of the hand finishes uppermost.

2a Try to coordinate the entire movement so that everything stops at the same moment: the step forward; the hip and shoulder rotation to the front; the explosive forward motion of the punch; the snap back of the opposite fist to the hip; the locking straight of the rear knee (vital!). This wi give your technique power and crispness

Reverse punch *Bandae jireugi*

The reverse punch is similar in every respect to the forward punch, except that this time the fist opposite to the extended foot is employed. Often the reverse punch will be more powerful than the forward punch, as the opportunity exists to generate even more hip action – and therefore torque – in its preparation. For this reason, it is the preferred technique for students practising kyukpa.

Hints and tips

- Practise stepping forward concentrating on the correct rotation of your hips through the punch.
- Be careful not to over-extend your punching shoulder in an effort to reach your target.
- Remember to grip your fist tightly at the moment of impact.

* SIDE VIEW

1 This time prepare by drawing your hips back as you place the left punching fist on your hip and raise your right arm in front of you for the reaction move.

2 Step forward into long stance – again, with your right foot – as you snap your right fist back to your hip and your left fist out to the target. Square your body as you did before and check that your weight is spread evenly across both feet, with your body upright.

2a Once again, your target here is the solar plexus, so check that your punching knuckles are extended correctly, and don't be tempted to punch too high.

Backfist side strike *Deungjumeok yeop chigi*

This is extremely effective as a close-range attack either to a front- or side-facing target. Contact is made with a closed fist using the knuckles of the first and second finger only. This concentrates the force into a smaller surface area, resulting in a far more powerful attack. To achieve this position you need to bend the wrist just enough so as not to connect with the flat part of the back of the hand.

Hints and tips

- Bring the fists into line with the opposing elbow as you prepare to deliver. This ensures that you are fully loaded for the strike while remaining on the target line.
- Don't let your rear knee fall inward when applying the hip twist, or your stance will lose form and weaken.

1 Raise both arms up to shoulder height as you pull your hips back, ready for launching your attack. Your forearms should be parallel – striking arm uppermost – with your striking (right) fist facing away from you and the opposite fist facing down.

2 Step forward into back stance and strike out, keeping your attacking arm bent at the elbow while snapping the rear fist to your hip. Keep your stance strong and side-on, to prevent over-rotation of the shoulders.

2a Note the bend in the striking wrist. There is no need to extend the fist beyond the line of your body when you finish the strike, as the combined action of both arms and hip twist generates the explosive action required. To do otherwise will only lead to a push. Targets are high-section and rib areas.

Backfist front strike *Deungjumeok ap chigi*

This is a variation of the previous strike, and is used for attacks to the front instead of to the side. The start position is the same for both. Try to think of driving the elbow downwards, to add force to the fist as it extends into the finished position. Targets are usually high section, and largely depend on your position in relation to the opponent.

Hints and tips

- Don't over-extend your arm or you will lose power. Instead, keep your attacking arm bent at the elbow by ensuring that you are closer to your target.

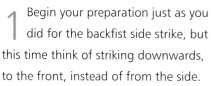

★ FRONT VIEW

1 Begin your preparation just as you did for the backfist side strike, but this time think of striking downwards, to the front, instead of from the side.

2 Again, step forward into back stance and strike, snapping the rear fist back to your hip. Lead with your attacking elbow and your fist will follow a true line of attack to your intended target. As before, you are striking with the back of the knuckles, so make sure your wrist is slightly bent.

2a Again, when viewed from the front you can see the alignment of the body on completion of the attack, which is in this case directed to the bridge of the nose. The prominent knuckles are turned downwards, as the impact comes from above, with the elbow finishing directly beneath.

Low block *Arae makki*

The low-section block is typically used to deflect an attack that is directed towards your groin – an example being the front kick. However, it can also be effective during sparring as a defence against body kicks directed to the lower part of your trunk. You can perform this move with either arm, in any stance and with the hand open or closed (both are shown here). For open hand, contact is made with the outside edge of your straightened hand (*sonnal*), and for closed hand contact is made with the outside edge of your forearm (*palmok*). As with all blocking techniques, the emphasis should be on the correct application of the hips to ensure that sufficient power is generated to make the block effective.

Hints and tips

- Note how the long stance is not shown until the completion of the block. To incorporate the hip action fully, it is necessary to turn to the side during preparation. As you twist your hips to the front in an explosive action, you will be able to fix your stance at the same time as you finish the blocking action.
- Don't turn your head away from your opponent at any time during your twist to the side. Keep looking forward and concentrating throughout to be sure you have not misread your opponent's kick.
- Keep your opposite fist firmly closed and your elbow in, as this is a common oversight that leads to sloppy technique.

▲ CAUTION

- *Remember: in a self-defence situation someone is trying to damage you when they kick at you, so it's vital that you train to make the block work for you. That means – as always – using your entire body to execute the technique.*

1 Place your left leg forward, then prepare the block by raising both arms up to the right side of your face. Cross your wrists with your right fist facing outward and your blocking arm closest to you, fist facing in. Remember to turn your hips to the right at this stage to coil yourself up, as this will help you to 'throw' your block out. You are now in the correct position to execute a strong and balanced movement with both arms.

* FRONT VIEW

$2a$ In this front view of knifehand block, you can see that the hand is directly over the knee in the finished position, thus ensuring that you have completely intercepted the kick before it extends beyond your front leg (in other words, closer to you). There is no need to pass your arm beyond the line of your body, as the emphasis should be on 'striking' the kicking leg rather than pushing it away.

OPEN-HAND VARIATION

2 Now snap your right fist down and back to your hip, rotating it at the same time as delivering the block with your left arm. The left fist should now be over your left knee and facing down, with the elbow soft (not locked). Remember that to make it powerful you need to turn your body to the front as you block. Lock your back knee straight and ensure that your feet are shoulder-width apart for stability.

Everything about the knifehand block (*hansonnal arae makki*) is the same, bar the now-open hand on the blocking arm. This means you can reach lower, as you are making contact with the side of the hand instead of the forearm. You may prefer to use this variation when in one of the shorter, more upright stances. Try it for yourself and see.

Inward block   *Momtong bakat palmok makk*

The his is the basic blocking technique used for defence against attacks to the middle section of the trunk. It uses the outer part of the forearm (*bakat palmok*) along the line of the little finger, and is delivered across the body from outside to in. It is therefore often referred to as outer forearm inward block, and is equally suitable for defence against either hand or foot attack as it can be very powerful when applied correctly. The basic application should be thought of as driving the elbow in a circular motion, from high up at the side of the body down and inward, towards the front, keeping the fist above and slightly forward of the elbow.

Hints and tips

- This is an easy block to cheat with and I have seen many students try to get away with merely flicking the fist forward from the shoulder with a little bit of hip twist. Don't do it! You'll only pay for your mistake when you realize that your block is too weak to adequately deflect any reasonable kick.

CLOSED HAND

1 Start by stepping forward with your left foot, pulling your left arm up to the left side, fist level with your face (palm-side out) and elbow as high as you can manage. Bring your opposite arm forward and rotate your hips to the left ready for the full body action of the block.

2 From here, everything needs to be done in one explosive action. Throw your blocking arm down and around, elbow first, to the finished position by pulling your opposite fist to your right hip as you simultaneously thrust the left side of your hips forward and assume back stance.

Hints and tips

- Try to ensure that your arm remains bent at an angle of about 90 degrees, with your hand level with your shoulder at completion. You should then find that your elbow travels furthest and finishes down close to your hip or belt (this is how you achieve the extra power). This means that as the blocking motion comes across your body, an attack directed anywhere between your hips and shoulder (middle section) will be intercepted. Remember – if your hand is too high, the risk of a kick slipping under your block and reaching its target is far greater.

*SIDE VIEW

OPEN HAND

1 The open-hand variation works particularly well with this block. Here, you can see how the body is fully loaded by turning to the left, ready to unleash the blocking action. This time the emphasis is on the open hand coming down to strike at the attacker's punch.

2 Note that you should not try to over-extend beyond the line of your body with your block: think of striking at the attack, rather than pushing it away. Use a mirror to check your own position until you feel comfortable that you have turned far enough into the correct position.

2a For the open-hand block, finish with the fingertips level with your shoulders to connect with the knife-edge of the open hand. All other aspects are consistent with the forearm block.

Outward block *Momtong bakat makki*

Here we cover three variations of the middle-section outward block: knifehand (*sonnal*), outer forearm (or little-finger side – *bakat palmok*) and inner forearm (or thumbside – *an palmok*). These are conventionally used to defend against hand attacks to the body. Each begins from a similar position at the side of the body, but differs in the blocking hand beginning open for knifehand and closed for the forearm blocks, always with the fist turned the opposite way to the finish position. This encourages a twisting action in the forearm to promote a tighter, more controlled action as you connect with the chosen part of your arm.

OUTER-FOREARM VARIATION

KNIFEHAND / OUTER FOREARM

1 Prepare to block with your left arm by bring your arms up in front of your body and stepping forward onto your left foot, with your body side-on. Your forearms should be parallel, with the blocking arm beneath the rear, reaction arm. Open the blocking hand and turn the palm up.

2 Withdraw your rear fist to your hip as you form back stance and deliver the knifehand block (don't forget the twisting action). Finish with the elbow down as low as your hip and bent to 90 degrees. Your arm will now protect you against any mid-section attack, should you misjudge the height.

For outer forearm block, prepare just as before but with the fist closed (palm-side up). Deliver the block in the same way, keeping the elbow tucked in, and finish this time with the fist level with your shoulder.

Hints and tips

- Make it easier on yourself by practising these blocking actions in back stance, as before. This will help to ensure that you are not distracted from developing your application by stepping into different positions as you learn.
- A common mistake with these blocks is to reach out too far toward the attacker. If you think about this logically

you will realize that if you need to extend your arm then the attack is not a threat, as it will not reach you and therefore needn't worry you at all! Only when your opponent has judged the distance correctly will the attack be a problem, so keep your composure and your blocking arm sufficiently bent to enable the whole of your middle section to be covered by the action.

* FRONT VIEW

INNER FOREARM

1 This block differs at the start, as the fist now begins from a palm-down position. Keep both arms high at the beginning, as this helps you to generate more power as you drive the left elbow through to the final position.

2 Execute the block just as before, except that the twisting action in the wrist means you can now connect with the attack using the thumbside of your forearm.

2a This viewpoint shows how the body profile is completely side-on during this block, which will help you to protect your vulnerable target areas from attack. Again, watch for the tendency to over-extend the blocking arm outside of the line of your body, as this will throw you off balance.

High block *Eolgul makki*

Often referred to as rising block due to the upward action, this block can be used to protect against either a front attack directed towards your face or a downward attack from overhead. Choose between the forearm and knifehand to block with, but always make sure your blocking arm finishes close to your head and inclined slightly to deflect the attack away. As with all the blocking actions, think of them not as defence moves but as attacks. This will help you 'strike' at the arm of your opponent. Start out practising in long stance to build up your confidence, as the deep position gives you a greater feel of power in your movement.

* SEE ALTERNATIVE VIEW

KNIFEHAND VARIATION

1 Begin by turning your entire body to the right side as you prepare, crossing your arms with the left arm underneath and the fist upturned. Keep your body aligned vertically to get a good hip action; I have seen many students lean down to get under the attack – this throws your balance off and weakens the technique.

2 Take a deep step forward into long stance. Throw the block up and very slightly forward as you smartly withdraw your right arm until the fist rests upturned at the hip. For maximum force, time the block, the reaction, the hip twist and the step to finish simultaneously.

The principles are the same as for the forearm, with only two differences: open the blocking hand at the start of the preparation move to connect with the attack using the knifehand, and adjust the line of your blocking hand through the movement to keep your open hand rising up in front of your face. This ensures that you don't miss the attack.

2a Make a strong stance and keep your right elbow tucked in. Your body must not lean forward; instead, try to push your hips forward and to the front, and don't over-extend the blocking arm.

Hints and tips

- Note the start position of the rear arm for this block. Don't let it sit casually on your hip as you block; instead, reach forward (keeping the fist turned down) as you prepare to block. This will let you pull it sharply and powerfully back to your hip as you invert it, adding power and balancing the whole movement.

- Although you are turning your body to 'wind up' for a good block action, don't look away from the attack at any stage. You don't want to be fooled if your opponent tries to mask the real attack that is directed elsewhere.

- Remember not to over-extend in an effort to reach your chosen target. If you need to do this, you are too far away for the choice of technique. Move closer or choose another more suitable technique.

BLOCK/STRIKE COMBINATION

This is an advanced combination technique involving the high-section knifehand block with a simultaneous knifehand strike to the neck of the attacker *(jebipoom sonnal mok chigi)*. This is a good technique to use when stepping forward inside a high-section attack, as it affords you the element of surprise.

1 Prepare by rotating right, your left (blocking) arm positioned as before. This time, prepare your right arm for the knifehand strike by opening the hand and taking the arm up behind you; it should be bent at 90 degrees, with your forearm held vertically and the hand turned out.

2 Throw your hips in as you step forward. Bring your left arm up and across your face to deflect the attack, while at the same time striking firmly to the neck of your attacker with the right knifehand, rotating it to face upward and keeping your elbow slightly bent for control.

Palm heel block *Batangson makki*

This is a difficult block to perform well; practise it diligently to perfect the correct action. Concentrate on generating a good body action, as this is what drives the block out rather than a swing of the arm, which many lazy students try to get away with. Your grading examiner knows how it should be done and will be watching closely, so don't wait until then to find out you've been doing it wrong! Again, the basic principle is to strike at the attack, not push it away, so an explosive action is required for it to be effective. Two variations are shown here: the upward block defending against a middle-section punch, and the turning block defending against a kick.

＊ SIDE VIEW

UPWARD BLOCK

1 As soon as you begin to advance with your left foot, drop your left fist down towards the knee (palm down), with the opposite fist outstretched for the pull back that will serve as a strong reaction to the outward blocking action. Your hips should face forward, ready to rotate to the side on delivery.

2 Now, as you step forward and form back stance, do the following altogether as one action: throw your hips around to the right, smartly withdraw your right fist to your hip as you rotate it to face upwards, and turn your left hand up to make contact with the heel of your palm.

2a Finish with the palm of your blocking hand no higher than your shoulder, elbow tucked in. Keep your weight back on your rear foot in back stance and your body upright, hips and shoulders turned side-on to your opponent.

Hints and tips

- What is important here is the use of the opposing arm – to balance the blocking action – and a good strong hip rotation that throws the block into position. Do it well and you will find that the blocking arm actually travels only a very small distance from start to finish, but nevertheless achieves a great deal of force.
- Keep both elbows tucked in throughout the upward block movement. By keeping them close to your sides as they move, not only will your technique be crisp and compact, but you will also be bringing your blocking hand through the centre-line of your trunk. This will ensure that you intercept the punch being directed to your stomach, deflecting it out to the side, above your shoulder, instead of up into your face.

* SIDE VIEW

TURNING BLOCK

1 Begin with the blocking hand in position on the hip, the body coiled to the left and the opposite arm up for the reaction move. The blocking arm travels forward from the hip, not around in a circular motion: the turning action, and power, is achieved through the rotation of the hips as you step forward.

2 As you step into back stance, thrust the block forward using your hip action until your body is in a side-on position, palm heel level with the solar plexus. Your forearm will be almost horizontal (depending on the height of the attack). Pull the rear fist back hard to the hip to achieve a strong rotation.

2a Note how the block is not extended beyond the front foot and the body is turned completely side-on to the attack. This ensures that you remain in a balanced and comfortable position.

Cross-hand block _Eotgeoreo makki_

This is a powerful defence against kicking attacks to high, middle or low sections. Its strength comes from the introduction of the rear arm, which now supports the front arm (the front arm is always the one that corresponds with the leg that is placed in front). It is a versatile block as it also permits the use of either forearm or knifehand. The principle here is not to deflect the attack away, as is the intention with the single-arm blocks, but to stop the attack 'dead' before it reaches you. Begin practising with the low cross block using the forearms (_palmok eotgeoreo arae makki_), in long stance.

LOW BLOCK

1 Turn side-on to the right, and bring both fists to the start position at the hips. Keep looking forward as you prepare, but don't step too early, otherwise you will finish the stance before completing the block and lose much of your power.

2 As you step forward into left-foot long stance, punch down with both fists until they cross midway along the forearms, with the left arm in front.. Use plenty of hip action to give strength to the technique, being careful to fix a strong stance without leaning forward with your upper body.

HIGH BLOCK

1 For the crossing high-section block (_eotgeoreo eolgul makki_), begin from the same start position as before – side-on, fists by hips, except this time you will be punching upwards.

MIDDLE BLOCK

2 Step forward into long stance, punching up and across with your fists (left arm in front) as you twist to the front. Your forearms must finish above your forehead, stopping your opponent's overhead attack before it strikes you. Done correctly, you will see your opponent from beneath your arms.

1 Practise this in back stance using knifehand technique (*hansonnal eotgeoreo momtong makki*). Turn to the side, but this time open your hands (palms up) at the hip position. Keep looking at the attack and remain upright as you turn, only stepping forward when you are ready to throw the block out.

2 Step forward into back stance with your left leg as you thrust the open hands into position (left arm in front), to meet the attack wherever its trajectory dictates. Concentrate on meeting it with your hands rather than your arms.

Knifehand neck strike   *Sonnal mok chigi*

This attack uses the outside edge of the open hand in a typical chopping action. It may be performed in an inward or outward direction, and in this case is aimed to the neck. You can execute this technique equally well from a forward or reverse position and in any stance, so it is quite a useful strike to have in your arsenal. Both forward and reverse techniques are included here, so try practising both.

INWARD STRIKE

1 We're going to use the reverse technique here – this means stepping forward into left-leg long stance while executing a right-hand strike. Prepare by raising both arms up to shoulder level, left arm parallel to the ground and right arm up behind you. Bend both elbows to an angle of 90 degrees with only your right hand open (palm out). Load your hips by coiling to the right as your lead foot extends forward to take up the stance.

2 Step into long stance with the left foot and throw your hips forward as you strike in a circular motion with the right hand. Finish the technique turning the palm uppermost, and assist your body rotation by pulling your left fist sharply and powerfully to the left hip. Your body is now facing completely forward; all movements should finish together.

Hints and tips

- Make sure you stay relaxed during the movement, but remember that you must tighten your entire body at the moment of contact with your target. The knifehand must be fixed tightly to be of any use, so practise for speed without letting the hands go limp.
- Don't completely straighten your arm at the end of the strike, as this can cause injury to your elbow when you connect with a target that offers resistance. Practise striking a pad, ensuring that the palm of your hand finishes parallel to the floor, with your elbow slightly bent.

OUTWARD STRIKE

1 Now try the outward strike in a forward position – this means stepping with the same-side foot as the attacking arm (right). Turn to the left as you cross both arms up to the left side at head height, and with the striking hand open and closest to your face. By touching the backs of the wrists together in this start position, you will be able to rotate the rear fist as you pull it down to the hip when you strike.

2 As you step out into long stance with the right foot, thrust your hips around so that your body faces forward and strike out with the right knifehand, sharply withdrawing your rear fist to the left hip.

Elbow strike *Palkup chigi*

This is your most powerful upper-body weapon, capable of quite devastating results when used correctly. It is a popular choice of technique during exhibitions of breaking (*kyukpa* – more about this on page 136). Used on middle- and high-section targets, when in close to your opponent, the strike can be performed equally effectively in both forward and reverse positions, toward an attacker who is either behind or in front of you. There is plenty of choice, which makes it very practical in a variety of circumstances. Here we cover the front attack, where you strike horizontally to the middle section and upward to the high-section target.

* SEE ALTERNATIVE VIEW

MIDDLE-SECTION STRIKE

1 Prepare by twisting to the right and placing your right fist on your hip as you bring your opposite arm across the body at shoulder height for the reactionary pull back. Step forward with the left foot for a reverse technique, keeping your body turned side-on.

2 As your front foot touches down, snap your hips to the front and pull your left fist sharply to your hip. At the same time, throw your right elbow around to the centre of your body for the middle-section elbow strike (*palkup momtong chigi*). Keep your arm bent as though you are punching to your opposite shoulder. Turn the fist down and keep your upper body straight as you form the long stance.

* SIDE VIEW

MIDDLE-SECTION STRIKE

1a Here you can see how the body remains side-on as you step forward. Note how both fists are turned the opposite way to the finish position. This helps to achieve a more crisp delivery as you rotate the wrists of each hand to complete the attack. Apply this principle to all your blocks and strikes for sharper techniques.

Hints and tips

- Don't let the heel of your back foot lift up when you strike, as you need a well-balanced and firm base for such a powerful technique. This common mistake is caused by failing to lock your hips into position, and by allowing your back knee to relax and bend.

- Practise against a pad in order to fully appreciate the force that can be achieved with this technique. It will also help you to understand the important role your stance plays in the success of your strike.

HIGH-SECTION STRIKE

1 For the high-section strike *(palkup olryeo chigi)*, prepare as before, only this time you will be driving your elbow upwards rather than around from the side.

2 As you step into long stance with your left leg, thrust your right fist up to your right ear, which brings your attacking elbow up through the correct line. Finish with your fist turned palm-in, and your elbow level with your face.

Backward elbow strike *Palkup dwit chigi*

This technique is used against an opponent who attacks from behind. Your stance will be short – usually back stance or walking stance. If you have practised and developed a strong reaction movement of the non-attacking arm in previous techniques, then you will have the makings of a good strike here. This technique is only performed with the arm that corresponds to the rear leg, and your target will be either middle or high section.

MIDDLE-SECTION STRIKE

1 Begin by looking behind and reaching back with your right leg to take up a back stance. As you do this, raise your right arm out to the front in a forward punching position. Now place your left hand on top of the fist. This will help you to develop power by reinforcing the striking arm. Keep your hips facing the front at this stage in the technique.

2 Now transfer your body weight onto the right leg to form back stance as you thrust your right elbow in to its target, pushing with your left hand. This action resembles the pulling back of the arm when blocking or striking with the other hand. As you begin the strike, your right fist rotates so that the palm finishes face-up and the opposite hand moves to the front of the right fist to help drive the elbow in.

Hints and tips

- For extra power, leave your hips facing the front until the moment you transfer your body weight onto the back foot, and try to finish your stance and your strike together.
- Don't over-extend with the middle-section strike. Your fist should be tucked in to your hip at the finish point, so you will need to be close to your target for this strike to work.

* BACK VIEW

HIGH-SECTION STRIKE

1 For the high-section strike, begin the same as for middle section: right leg back, ready to transfer into back stance, and your striking arm out in front with your opposite hand on top of the fist.

2 As you transfer your weight back and pull your hips into the strike, drive your elbow back and upward to the target, finishing with both forearms forming a straight line. The fist remains palm-down throughout the strike, and the opposite hand rotates to a vertical position to reinforce the driving action.

2a Your body should remain upright and side-on as you execute the strike, with the point of the elbow extended furthermost. Eye contact with the opponent should be maintained throughout; don't be tempted to turn away at the moment of impact.

Spearhand thrust *Pyeonsonkeut chireugi*

Here, and overleaf, we look at the different ways to perform this strike to the three target areas: low, middle and high sections. Your attack is always aimed at a soft target such as the abdomen, the solar plexus or the throat. Practise the hand shape before trying this technique, otherwise you will injure yourself if you have not developed a strong hand position. For conditioning, I recommend practising striking into the palm of your other hand, making sure that all three longest fingers connect at the same time. Start softly and build up to a forceful strike over time, as this is an advanced technique for more experienced students.

▲ CAUTION

- *Due to their softer bones, children should not use this technique against real targets, even for practice purposes.*
- *A word of warning for adults: keep your fingernails cut short, otherwise not only will you risk injury to yourself but also to your training partners, by potentially spreading infection if you break the skin with this technique.*

LOW-SECTION STRIKE

1 Prepare to strike low section by turning your hips to the right as you step forward with the left leg to make a long stance. Raise your right arm up to your face with the hand open, palm facing down. At the same time, extend your left arm forward for the reaction.

2 Transfer your weight forward as you assume long stance. Throw your hips in to add the power as you pull your left fist to your right shoulder and thrust your striking hand forward to the low-section target. Keep your upper body vertical, and rotate your striking hand at the delivery of the move.

Hints and tips

- For low-section strike, imagine that your reaction arm is reaching out to grab at your opponent's clothing, then pull it sharply toward yourself as you strike. You will soon feel the additional power in your technique as you develop a coordinated movement.

HIGH-SECTION TARGET

HIGH-SECTION STRIKE

1 Again prepare by stepping forward with the left foot as you twist right, but this time with your open (right) hand at your hip, palm up. Raise your opposing arm up, bent at the elbow to aid your rotation and help balance the movement as you strike. Don't form the stance too early or you will lose power.

2 When your front foot is in position, throw your hips in and pull your left fist smartly to your hip as you strike out – in a similar way to a punch – with your right hand. Your target is the throat, so don't aim unrealistically high. Again, rotate the striking hand at the last moment, to finish palm-down.

Take care when practising high-section technique with a partner. It's no fun receiving a poorly controlled strike in the throat, so judge your distance carefully.

73

Middle spearhand strike *Pyeonsonkeut seweo chireug*

In the spearhand techniques on the previous page, the attacking hand was facing palm down for the high-section strike, and palm up for the low-section strike. In the next two sequences the strike is performed mid-section with the palm facing sideways. The first, and easier, of the two sequences is a straightforward strike to the solar plexus, hence the vertical position of the open hand, while the second variation shows how to perform a combined blocking action with the opposite hand as the counter-attacking strike is delivered. Practise the single strike first.

1 This strike can be performed in a forward or reverse position; the reverse is shown here. Load your technique by twisting to the right with your open (right) hand at the hip, palm up, and the left fist closed, up at shoulder level for the reaction. Take a deep step forward with the left foot for a long stance.

2 Form your long stance by throwing your hips forward at the same time as pulling your left fist sharply to your hip and thrusting your right spearhand to the centre target. Keep the forward knee out, your rear leg locked straight and your left elbow tucked in for a strong position.

BLOCK/STRIKE COMBINATION

The resulting time saved by using this attack as a counter-strike to a punch directed to your stomach area increases your chances of success, since only one combination action is performed instead of two separate moves. This action can also be performed just as effectively in the forward position (here, this would mean with the right leg forward).

Hints and tips

- The timing of your combined arm movements is important here, as they need to move in unison; however, to end in the correct position your left arm must move *slightly* ahead in order to finish under your opposite elbow.

- Don't lift your left elbow too high at the start, otherwise you will not be able to intercept the punch in the diagonal fashion required to throw it clear of your body.

1 Here, the start position of the left hand differs to the single strike. You will be using the open palm to deflect the punch that is coming towards your stomach, so open your left hand from the beginning and raise it vertically to head height as you step forward.

2 This time, as you throw your hips around to form the stance, strike across and down with your left palm heel before your opponent's punch reaches you. Thrust your right spearhand strike out as before, finishing with your left (open) hand horizontal, beneath your right elbow.

Ridgehand strike *Sonnal deung*

The ridgehand needs a lot of practice to be effective, as it is quite a difficult strike to perform properly. It uses the side edge of the open hand, along the line of the forefinger knuckle. To avoid injury, ensure that your thumb is tucked well under the palm, while maintaining a stiff hand by keeping the knuckles completely flat. It is used for high-section targets, and can be executed in any stance. I recommend that you learn it from a reverse long stance, as this will give you the best feedback on the success of your early practice.

Hints and tips

- Don't try to strike in an upward diagonal line, as you could easily catch the shoulder of your opponent rather than your intended target, especially when aiming to connect with the side of the neck. Instead, draw an imaginary arc over and slightly down with the attack.

- If you put all your effort into the arm movement, you will tend to throw your upper body off centre, so it ends up leaning, so concentrate on developing a strong hip action to launch the strike to the target.

1 Turn to the right as you extend your left foot forward. Prepare the left arm parallel to the floor at shoulder level, and reach behind and down with your right hand, palm turned up.

2 Now snap your hips to the front and rotate your upper body into the forward position by pulling your left fist to your hip as you form the long stance. Turn your striking hand over to face palm down as you bring it in an arc to the target. Upon completion, your ridgehand will be slightly inclined downwards from the horizontal position.

Palm heel strike _Batangson teok chigi_

This is the same hand shape as the earlier palm heel block (see page 62), and is used here as a forward-thrusting attack to either mid- or high-section targets. Good flexibility in the wrists is required for this technique to work, as you need to be able to pull your fingers out of the way of the heel of your hand so that they do not interfere with your striking point. Practise the strike from any stance, in either forward or reverse positions.

Hints and tips

- The action of this strike is almost identical to the conventional punch, except that the hand shape makes the attack shorter. You therefore need to bear this in mind when you set up for the strike, and begin closer to your intended target.

1 Extend your left foot forward and rotate your body right as you prepare your arms for both the strike and complementary reaction: left arm at shoulder level in front, and right arm tucked in, ready to strike. Remember to open your attacking hand at the start and maintain an upright position.

2 Form long stance by rotating your hips and shoulders to the front as you throw your strike forward and pull your left fist back to the hip, rotating both wrists at the finish position.

Front kick *Ap chagi*

The front kick is used primarily in one-step sparring (*hanbon kyurugi*), self-defence (hosinsul), breaking (kyukpa) and patterns (poomsae). Legitimate targets are anywhere from the lowest point (shins) upwards. It is not widely used in competition sparring as the likelihood of incurring a penalty from inadvertent contact to your opponent's lower body makes it a high-risk attack. It is generally performed from the back foot, as this enables the greatest amount of hip action to add power to the kick. From start to finish, your foot should move in a straight line. This makes it a very fast kick to execute – and therefore difficult to defend against, as there is little time to respond. Use the ball of the foot to connect.

Hints and tips

- Watch that the heel of your supporting foot doesn't lift up. Keep the foot flat on the floor through the kick, as this will give you the stability you need for an effective strike.

1 Practise from the guarding position, as this presents the least difficulty when learning to kick. Make sure that your back foot has a clear route past your front leg to your intended target, otherwise the kick will be thrown off course from the start.

2 Pivot your supporting foot out slightly to help with your balance as you bring your kick-side hip forward and your knee up to the front, beginning to form the foot shape with the left foot. Don't let your upper body tip to the side; instead, lean back slightly to let the hips through and maintain a covered position with your arms.

JUMPING FRONT KICK

The jumping variant of this kick (twieo ap chagi) is performed either by springing up from both feet, or by leaping from the front leg in a running motion. As with all of the jumping kicks, it is used for high kicking during demonstrations of breaking or one-step sparring.

FRONT VIEW

3 Continue to push your hips forward as you now extend your lower leg out to the chosen target, connecting with the ball of the foot. If you have limited flexibility, bend the supporting knee slightly, as this will help to extend the kick-side hip and give more reach and height to the kick.

3a Here you can see the alignment of the upper body – vertical, but tilting back slightly to allow the hips to move through and the fists to remain close in to the body. Keep your elbows tucked in.

4 As soon as the kicking leg is fully extended, bend the knee to bring your foot back down to the opposite knee. This will protect your knee against the jarring action of an uncontrolled over-extension, and also preserve your balance, enabling you to move efficiently into the next position.

Turning kick *Dollyo chagi*

There are two ways of executing this kick, each for a different purpose. The first uses the instep, or top of the foot (*baldeung*), and follows a forward, diagonal line to the target. It is commonly used in sparring, as most students find it easier to perform with success (little warning is given, due to the kick's tremendous speed). The second variation uses the ball of the foot, but in the foot-sword shape. This kick comes around to the target in a much wider circular movement, and is used for breaking due to its superior power. Both kicks may be performed from the front or rear leg, but rear is best as it allows you to generate far more hip action.

INSTEP KICK

1 Start in a right-leg back stance, assuming a guarding position as though you were facing a sparring partner. Now imagine in your mind's eye the path that your kicking foot will take to the target: forward and diagonally upward as you twist your kick-side hip forward.

2 Begin the kick by thrusting your right hip forward and transferring all your weight onto your supporting leg as you bring your right knee to the front. This will cause the knee to point inward slightly, which is going to throw the foot in from an angle – thus giving the kick its characteristic turning action.

3 Complete your body turn by pivoting on your supporting foot. This will allow you to rotate your hips fully, giving you the added power that will make the kick powerful. Extend your foot to the target, connecting with the instep.

JUMPING TURNING KICK

The jumping turning kick (*twieo dollyo chagi*) is performed in the same way as the jumping front kick, and looks spectacular when used during demonstrations of Taekwondo for breaking boards held overhead.

Hints and tips

- To make the kick harder for your opponent to defend against, think of your knee acting like a spring that recoils as soon as the foot reaches the target. Done correctly, without dropping the knee, the foot will then bounce back to touch your rump before your partner has a chance to block.
- Don't lean over to the side – a common mistake with beginners. By maintaining a more in-line position with your upper body, you will be able to generate far more power from your hip thrust. You will also benefit from improved balance, which will help you to recover following your attack.

BALL-OF-FOOT KICK

2 For this more powerful turning kick, begin from the same guarding position as before, with the right foot back. Now raise the kicking leg up to the side, keeping the knee bent and your whole leg on one plane level with your hips. Make the correct foot shape for a strike using the ball of your foot.

3 Now lean backwards and pivot round on your supporting foot, allowing your hips to come through as you accelerate the knee to the front and straighten out your leg for the kick. Aim to finish slightly beyond the centre position, thereby ensuring that you kick through your target with full force.

Chop kick *Naeryu chagi*

The basic principle of this attack is to raise the foot as high as possible and then bring it forcefully down onto the target. It is delivered with either the underside of the foot or rear of the heel, and can be applied with front or rear foot, incorporating a turning, spinning or skipping action to generate added power. As the leg must be raised before descending, the supporting leg will usually be back on the floor before the kick reaches its target. The jumping leg chop, therefore, is not covered here.

* SEE ALTERNATIVE VIEW

1 Prepare to kick high-section using the rear foot by taking a guarding stance with the right leg back, eyes focused on the target.

2 Begin the move by thrusting the right hip forward to accelerate the leg upwards to maximum height. The leg may be bent at the knee for greater speed at this point. Pivot the supporting foot out and lean back slightly to allow the kick-side hip to move forward.

3 As the foot reaches full height, straighten the leg out for maximum reach, but without locking the joint fully (to protect the knee joint on impact). Keep the supporting foot firmly on the floor and bring the striking foot down onto the target as quickly and forcefully as possible.

* FRONT VIEW

3a Don't allow the supporting foot to rise off the ground during the upward momentum of the kick. This will cause instability and lead to your foot coming out from underneath you at the moment of impact.

Hints and tips

- Avoid swinging your arms, or excessive movement of the upper body, during this kick, as this can signal your intention to your opponent.
- Don't become complacent with a well-executed kick: your opponent may have anticipated your move, so you will need a good recovery to protect against a counter-attack.

▲ CAUTION

- *To avoid possible injury, be sure that you warm up and stretch out thoroughly before attempting this high kick.*

4 Be careful not to let your foot hit the floor as the kick follows through – this is likely if you transfer too much weight forward while bringing the kick down. Note the fully rotated position of the hips at this point compared to the starting position. This is essential to achieve maximum power.

5 Land as quickly as you can in a guarding position, with the kicking foot in front or behind according to the situation.

Side kick *Yeop chagi*

This is an extremely valuable kick to have in your repertoire, as it can be useful in so many situations. Using the side edge of the foot – the foot sword (*balnal*) – you can block against an opponent's kick by striking at the shin; deliver a disabling kick to the front or side of the knee; administer a 'checking' strike to the hip/midriff of the advancing opponent; and execute a conventional attack to the face.

You can step forward and kick, skip and kick from the front foot, spin backwards or jump up to kick – all extremely powerfully. Follow these essential basics to get the most from this kick.

*SEE ALTERNATIVE VIEW

1 Begin in a right-leg-back guarding position. Your plan here is to bring your right foot in front of the left, forward and up to strike high section.

2 Now throw your right hip forward and raise the kicking foot to the front of the opposite knee. At the same time, change your guard so that your right shoulder is forward.

3 Continue the hip twist by pivoting your standing foot to point to the rear as you continue to raise and extend your right foot up and out towards the target. When the leg is fully extended, your upper body should lean backwards to maintain your balance, with your arms close to your chest.

JUMPING SIDE KICK

The jumping side kick (*twieo yeop chagi*) can be performed by springing off both feet from a standing position, or from either foot during a stepping or running action. Tuck your trailing leg up toward your groin to maintain tension throughout your entire body.

* FRONT VIEW

3a Once again, the emphasis is on making sure that you do not lean around your kicking leg, or you will lose all your potential power by bending at the hips. Look along your right shoulder, hip, knee and foot for a straight line.

4 Don't flop the leg down in front after the kick, or you will run the risk of walking onto a counter-punch (or similar). Instead, snap the foot immediately back to the body. You now have the balance to move equally well in any direction.

Hints and tips

- Perform the complete action in a continuous motion, without pausing at the different stages of the kick. Again, use your knee as a spring to recoil the foot back to your body as soon as you have achieved full extension of the leg.

Back kick *Dwit chagi*

The back kick is one of Taekwondo's most powerful kicks, often stopping the opponent's advance completely when employed in sparring and competition matches. Used during technical exchanges as your opponent steps in to launch an attack, it can have devastating results, as it is both fast and very strong. In addition, since the initial body-turn makes it look similar to the high-section hook kick, it is extremely difficult to interpret before it reaches its target. Practise this kick against a solid resistance pad until it becomes a reflex action when your opponent throws a kick off the rear foot. You will then have a formidable weapon that you can unleash – often before your opponent can react in time to evade it.

Hints and tips

- Begin the spin with the hip rotation, followed by your head. This will add the much-needed speed to your twist before you extend the kicking leg.
- If you find it difficult to maintain balance with this kick, try bending the supporting knee a little and leaning down further.
- Whatever height you choose, don't allow your hips to turn toward the kick, as this will place you in a more sideways position, with the kicking foot pointing out to the side instead of down, and you will reveal more of your own target areas to your opponent.

1 Begin in guarding stance, with the right foot back, and visualize your target as being directly in front at mid-section height. Plan to connect with the bottom of your right heel just above the belt of your opponent or sparring partner.

2 Pivot 180 degrees on the ball of your left foot, pivoting your hips in a clockwise direction and transferring your weight onto your supporting leg. Lift your kicking foot to the supporting knee, tucking your kicking knee in towards your body.

JUMPING BACK KICK

The jumping back kick (*twieo dwit chagi*) is a great point-scorer in competition. When you jump from either or both feet, try to extend the trailing leg in the opposite direction to the kick, and remain facing away from the target, as this encourages tension in the body at the moment of contact. This leads to a more forceful attack.

3 Thrust out the kicking leg as swiftly as you can, while leaning down with your upper body to maintain balance and help you drive the kick out. Judge your distance from the target so that you connect well before the leg is fully extended.

4 Smartly withdraw your foot until your knees almost touch. This will enable you to regain your composure, maintain your balance and place you in a comfortable position to be able to evade a counter-strike or follow up your back kick with another appropriate move.

5 If all is well, you can then step down with the right foot, turning your body to assume a guarding position once more, ready to continue.

Hook kick *Huryeo chagi*

This is a favourite kick for many Taekwondo students and instructors alike. It has all the finesse and grace that so often impresses the onlooker, with deadly speed and power. Use it with either the rear of the heel (*dwitkumchi*) for breaking, or the underside of the extended foot (*balkeut*) for sparring. Whether performed from the front or rear leg, either with or without spinning first, it is a very difficult kick for your opponent or training partner to evade.

1 Take up the usual right-leg-back guarding stance and rehearse in your mind the reverse spin to kick with the rear foot.

2 Begin by pivoting clockwise on your front foot and pushing your hips forward and around *without* leaning in with your head as you transfer the weight from your right foot. Keep looking ahead.

3 Continue rotating clockwise, then quickly turn your head to look over your right shoulder. Once the supporting foot has pivoted 180 degrees, to point away from the target, keep it flat on the floor. Raise and begin to straighten the kicking leg as fast as you can while turning; this combined motion generates the characteristic whip-like action.

JUMPING HOOK KICK

As with the jumping back kick, this technique produces devastating results when used with the jump (*twieo huryeo chagi*). Keep your hips under your body instead of leaning forward from the waist for this move, and lift the trailing leg in the opposite direction for increased tension on contact.

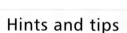

Hints and tips

- Practise on a soft pad at low level to develop confidence in the turning action of this kick. Only increase the height as you become more competent with the spinning motion of the body.
- Be careful not to land heavily after this kick, as this could make you an easy target for a counter-strike from your opponent. Practise completing the technique by landing with the kicking foot both in front and behind.

4 Whipping the kicking leg in from the side, connect with your target using the underside of the extended foot. The supporting leg should remain straight and your upper body in line with the kicking leg, leaning back for balance.

5 With the heel of your supporting foot down firmly on the floor, you have an ideal brake with which to control your over-spin. Continue the motion of the kicking leg by bending the knee until the heel comes all the way around to your rear.

Poomsae

Poomsae is the collective name given to the series of movements performed in a predefined sequence by students from beginner to Black Belt and beyond. These sequences are designed to simulate both defence and counter-attacking movements, performed against multiple imaginary opponents from different directions, and using a diverse range of Taekwondo techniques. This kind of practice supplements other types, such as sparring, breaking and basic drill training, by combining the techniques and movements in a logical and rhythmical chain. Practised correctly, they allow the student to express the beautiful and dynamic side of Taekwondo, while at the same time developing – among other positive skills – the coordination, timing, balance and concentration of the performer. As with the basic techniques, to truly master poomsae requires many

hundreds of hours of repeated practice. Therefore, in pursuit of the perfect performance, one learns the true meaning of patience, self-control and perseverance.

YOUR POOMSAE SEQUENCES

In this section I have chosen to include three specific examples of Taegeuk poomsae from the series of eight that takes the beginner up to Black Belt, each sequence progressively more difficult and complex than the last. They have been broken down into their respective recognized number of movements, but I have also included further transitional stages to make the sequences easier to follow here. The recognized moves are indicated by a number that corresponds to the 'path' diagram, helping you to visualize the path of movement and orientate yourself correctly.

You will be introduced to the first sequence from an early stage in your training career, and will be expected to practise it repeatedly until you are able to perform it confidently and to a sufficient standard for promotion to the next grade. You will then be instructed in the next in the sequence of Taegeuk, and so it will continue until you reach the rank of 1st Keup (red belt with black bars).

TAEGEUK IL-JANG (NO.1)
The first sequence is called Taegeuk Il-Jang (No.1) and is required learning for the White Belt student. This poomsae represents 'Heaven and Light' and symbolizes the beginning, or creation of all things. Consisting of eighteen movements, it is intended to be uncomplicated, and is so designed to introduce you to the principle of poomsae training. It incorporates only the most basic techniques that you will have learned from your first lessons, and is performed in just two different stances: long stance and walking stance. Taegeuk Il-Jang lays the solid foundation from which your Taekwondo abilities will grow.

TAEGEUK SA-JANG (NO.4)

The second sequence I have chosen to include is Taegeuk Sa-Jang (No.4) and is required for those wishing to promote to 5th Keup (green belt with blue bars). Taegeuk Sa-Jang represents 'Thunder', and symbolizes great power and destructive force. This often promotes fear, and so teaches us to be calm and brave when facing danger, for just as quickly as thunder arrives, so it passes and everything returns to normal. This sequence has twenty movements and involves more advanced double-handed techniques and hand/foot combinations. It requires the student to concentrate on emphasizing strength generated from within to be truly effective, due to the resulting abbreviated body movements.

TAEGEUK PAL-JANG (NO.8)

The final sequence included here is Taegeuk Pal-Jang (No.8). Pal-Jang is required learning for Red Belt students of 1st Keup. It represents 'Earth' and is symbolic of the creative force from which all things grow. It consists of twenty-four movements and, as one would expect from the final Taegeuk, contains the most advanced techniques and combinations of the series. At this stage in your training, you will have accumulated a great deal of Taekwondo knowledge to complement your physical expertise, and it is important that you have a mature, responsible attitude toward your extraordinary abilities. Calm, controlled breathing is essential if this poomsae is to be performed with the grace and elegance expected from the most senior student prior to becoming a Black Belt holder.

KEEP PRACTISING

Practise your poomsae regularly and earnestly, never neglecting the earlier ones in the series. In your progression through the colour-belt ranks, this defines the exceptional student from the mediocre one. A Taekwondo Master can and will be able to judge much about you by the standard of your poomsae performance. And, since this aspect of Taekwondo

FOLLOWING THE STEPS

For ease of reference, a front-view perspective is shown for all moves, or sequences of moves, that are performed facing the opposite direction (in other words, with the back to camera). Every time a sequence of moves such as this begins, this is indicated by a front-view panel, and all subsequent steps are labelled as front view until the perspective once again returns to normal. If in any doubt, check the diagram in the top-left corner to make sure that you are moving in the right direction.

represents sixty per cent of your final pass mark in promotional tests, you would be unwise to overlook the significance of superior poomsae training.

Taegeuk 1 • *Il-Jang*

This is the first poomsae in the series that takes the beginner through to the coveted Black Belt. Consisting of eighteen moves, it is further broken down here for easier understanding of the transitional steps. As you would expect from the first in the series, the techniques performed are the most basic. Try to remember the finer

Ready stance (*chumbi seogi*)

✳ START

1a From the ready position, look left and prepare your arms for left-arm low-section block. Keep your hips facing the front until you execute the blocking action.

❶

1b Pivot left on the toes of your right foot and the heel of your left foot; this will keep you on your line and set you into walking stance. Throw your hips round as you deliver the block.

❷

2 Pull back with your right hip and fist to load for the next punch before stepping forward into walking stance. As you step, execute a right-fist mid-section punch, thrusting your hips round.

❺

5b Step to the front into left-leg long stance and use your hips to throw the blocking arm out.

❻

6 Load your next attack by pulling the right hip and fist back ready to punch, without stepping, then execute a right-fist reverse punch to the mid-section.

❼

7a Now look to your right as you prepare your arms for a left-outer-forearm inward block, drawing your rear foot up before stepping.

❼

7b Step to your right into right-leg walking stance and deliver a reverse mid-section inward block with the left outer forearm.

details of their application as explained step by step earlier in the book, and this will raise the level of your performance. When you stand on your chosen mark to begin, visualize the shape of the pattern from beginning to end. You want to finish on the same spot, so pay attention to the sequence of steps that will enable you to do so.

3a Pivot clockwise on your left foot and turn to face the opposite direction as you prepare a right-arm low-section block. Look in the direction of your next movement before turning.

3b Step into a right-leg walking stance and deliver the low block. Feel that you are moving your entire body into the block as you complete the movement.

4 After first loading your hips, step forward to execute a left-fist mid-section punch in walking stance. Check that your shoulders are square to the front and you are not leaning forward.

5a Withdraw your front foot and look left towards the centre as you prepare to block low-section with the left arm. Keep your back straight and your hips side-on until you block.

8 Step forward into left-leg walking stance and execute a right-fist mid-section punch. Be sure to involve your hips for a strong punching action.

9a Look left, pivoting anti-clockwise on the rear foot and withdrawing your front foot as you prepare both arms for a right-arm mid-section inward block using the outer forearm.

9b Turn into left-leg walking stance and deliver the reverse block, throwing your hips to the centre position.

10 Step forward with the right leg into walking stance and execute left-fist reverse mid-section punch.

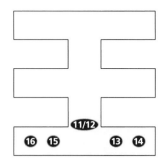

11/12
⑯ ⑮ ⑬ ⑭

11a Withdraw your front leg and look over your right shoulder to the centre line, while preparing your arms for a right-arm low-section block.

⑪

11b Step forward into long stance with your right foot, while twisting your hips forward and executing low-section block.

⑫

12 Remain in the same position and – loading your attack first – deliver a reverse mid-section punch with the left fist.

Hints and tips

• As the stance in Step 12 does not change from the previous move, remember to turn your hips out of position to load your punch before executing, otherwise you will have only the strength of your extending arm with which to strike.

⑭

14c Step down in front with your right foot as you deliver a mid-section punch with your right fist.

15a Turn clockwise by withdrawing the right foot and pivoting on the left. Look over your right shoulder early in your move and prepare to block high section with the right arm.

⑮

15b Throw your hips in as you deliver the block and step forward into right-leg walking stance.

16a Keep your arms in position as you thrust your kick-side hip in with your left-leg front kick.

13a Look left and draw your rear leg up as you prepare your arms for a left-arm high-section block. Keep your hips facing the front at this stage.

13b Step left into walking stance with the left foot and deliver the high-section block, now throwing your hips around.

14a Keep both hands in position while thrusting the right hip forward and executing right-leg front kick.

14b Withdraw your kicking foot to the opposite knee to retain your balance and composure, before pulling the right hip back for the next punch.

16b Withdraw your kicking foot back to the opposite knee – again, to retain balance – keeping your arms in position until you punch in the next move.

16c Pull back your hips before thrusting in with your left-fist mid-section punch as you step down into walking stance.

17a Pivot clockwise on your right foot and prepare a left-arm low-section block. Over-turn your hips so that you can snap them back in to assist the blocking action.

✳ FRONT VIEW

95

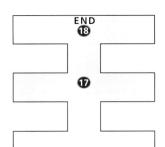

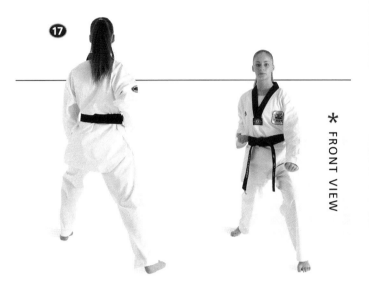

FRONT VIEW

17b Step into left-leg long stance and deliver the low-section block. Remember to step out with the front leg to prevent yourself wobbling with your technique.

Hints and tips

• Whenever you turn to face another direction, begin the move by pulling your hips out and rotating them toward the new direction. This will help you to gain the strength that makes the technique effective.

FRONT VIEW

18 Now step forward into right-leg long stance, and shout (*kihap*) as you execute a right-fist mid-section punch.

END

Turn your head to look over your left shoulder as you pivot anti-clockwise on your front foot, withdrawing your rear leg, and turn to face the front. Pull your fists to your hips and lift up onto the balls of your feet as you prepare to return to the ready position.

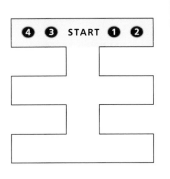
Taegeuk 4 • *Sa-Jang*

This is the fourth in the series of Taegeuks, and is performed by those testing for 5th Keup (Green belt, blue tags). It consists of twenty movements (again, here broken down into further transitional stages), having more complex hand and foot combinations than previous poomsae, and demands a greater degree

Ready stance (*chumbi seogi*)

★ START

1a Turn to face left while bringing the arms back ready to deliver twin-knifehand guarding block. Note the rotation of the palms of the hands.

1b Extend the left foot slightly to assume back stance and execute mid-section twin-knifehand guarding block.

2 Step forward into long stance with the right foot and execute mid-section spearhand thrust with the right hand while placing the left open-hand under the right elbow, palm down.

3a Pivot 180 degrees clockwise on the back foot to face the opposite direction, and prepare both arms ready to deliver twin-knifehand guarding block to the right.

3b Step into back stance and execute mid-section twin-knifehand guarding block.

4 Step forward into long stance with the left foot and execute mid-section spearhand thrust with the left hand while placing the right open-hand under the left elbow, palm down.

5a Pivot on the back foot, turning anti-clockwise to face the front while preparing both arms as in Step 1a.

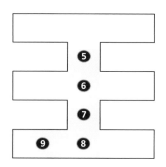

of balance and coordination to accomplish it with the finesse that your Grading Examiner will now be looking for. Correct rhythm becomes more important than before, as some of the techniques are grouped in combinations that involve only

5b Step into long stance with the left foot, executing high-section knifehand block with the left hand and inward knifehand strike with the right hand simultaneously.

6a Pivot the left foot outward and bring the right knee forward for front kick, while maintaining composure of the upper body.

6b Deliver the right-leg front kick.

6c Immediately bring the kicking foot back to the supporting leg to maintain balance.

8a Step forward with the left foot a distance equal to walking stance and then pivot slightly on the left foot, raising the right leg to the left knee to deliver side kick.

8b Execute a right-leg side kick, pivoting your supporting foot 180 degrees to the rear.

8c Immediately withdraw the leg to the opposite knee and retain balance while preparing to deliver mid-section twin-knifehand guarding block.

8d Step forward with the right foot into back stance and execute mid-section twin-knifehand guarding block.

one step. As always, turn your head to look in the direction of your next move before leaving the last position, and try to develop your speed and power without adversely affecting the smoothness with which you move between stances.

6d Step forward into long stance with the right leg and execute a left-hand mid-section punch.

7a Pivot slightly on your right foot as you raise your left foot to the right knee to prepare to deliver side kick.

7b Execute a left-leg side kick, pivoting your supporting foot 180 degrees to the rear.

7c Immediately withdraw the leg to the opposite knee, and retain balance before stepping down.

9a Turn to the left, looking over your left shoulder and pivoting 270 degrees anti-clockwise on your front foot, and prepare a mid-section outer-forearm outward block.

9b Step forward with the left foot into back stance and deliver the left-arm block.

10a Extend your right (kick-side) hip forward, pivoting the left (supporting) foot outward slightly as you perform a right-leg mid-section front kick.

10b Immediately withdraw the kicking foot to the opposite knee as you return to the upright position. This enables you to rotate your upper body more easily for the next move.

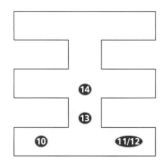

10c Prepare your arms for a right mid-section inward block in the same direction.

10d Step back with your right foot into back stance and execute the reverse block with the right arm.

11a Pivot 180 degrees clockwise on your left foot to face right, withdrawing your right foot. As your feet touch, prepare a mid-section outward block with the right outer forearm.

11b Step forward with the right foot into back stance and deliver the right-arm block.

13a Turn 90 degrees anti-clockwise, pivoting on your right foot, and prepare your arms for a left high-section knifehand block and simultaneous right high-section knifehand strike.

13b Step forward into long stance with your left foot and deliver the block/strike combination.

14a Maintain your upper body position as you turn your right side forward, bringing your right foot to the left knee for front kick.

✳ FRONT VIEW

✳ FRONT VIEW

Hints and tips

- The reverse blocking performed in walking and back stances is particularly difficult. It is important to place your feet slightly wider than you are used to doing, so that you can more easily retain your balance and an upright position through the techniques.

12a Pivot outward on your right (supporting) foot to allow your kick-side hip through as you execute a left-leg mid-section front kick.

12b Immediately withdraw the kicking foot to the opposite knee before preparing to block with your left arm.

12c Prepare both arms for a reverse mid-section inward block with the left inner forearm.

12d Execute the block with your left arm as you step back with your left foot into back stance.

* FRONT VIEW

14b Now lower your fists and execute right-leg front kick to the mid-section.

* FRONT VIEW

14c Immediately withdraw the kicking foot to the opposite knee and prepare a backfist strike with the right fist.

* FRONT VIEW

14d Step forward with the right foot into long stance and execute right high-section backfist front strike.

* FRONT VIEW

15a Draw your left foot towards the front leg as you turn to the left, preparing for mid-section inward block using the left outer forearm.

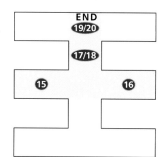

* FRONT VIEW

15b
Step into walking stance with the left foot and deliver the left-arm block.

* FRONT VIEW

15c
Without pausing, withdraw the blocking fist to the hip and execute a reverse mid-section punch with the right fist.

* FRONT VIEW

16a
Pivot 180 degrees clockwise on your left foot and prepare a mid-section inward block using the right outer forearm.

* FRONT VIEW

16b
Step into walking stance with the right foot and deliver the right-arm block.

* FRONT VIEW

18b
Now withdraw the right fist to your hip as you execute a forward mid-section punch with the left fist. (Perform these two punches in rapid succession.)

* FRONT VIEW

19a
Bring your rear foot forward and prepare to deliver a mid-section inward block using the right outer forearm.

* FRONT VIEW

19b
Step forward into long stance with the right foot and deliver the right-arm block.

* FRONT VIEW

20a
Remain in the same stance, withdrawing the right arm to the hip as you execute a reverse mid-section punch with the left fist.

Hints and tips

• Pay special attention to your hand positions through all the transitional movements and always keep the heel of your supporting leg firmly on the floor through the kicks. These points are so often neglected by students and consequently lead to sloppy performances by candidates going for promotion.

16 Without pausing, withdraw the blocking fist to the hip and execute a reverse mid-section punch with the left fist.

17a Turn 90 degrees to your left, pivoting on your right foot, and prepare a mid-section inward block using the left outer forearm.

17b Step forward into long stance with the left foot and deliver the left-arm block.

18a Remain in the same stance, withdrawing the left arm to your hip as you execute a reverse mid-section punch with the right fist.

20b Now withdraw the left fist to your hip as you execute a forward mid-section punch with the right fist. (Perform these two punches in rapid succession and also perform the *kihap*.)

Look over your left shoulder as you pivot anti-clockwise on your right foot, drawing your left foot around to form ready position once again, facing the front. Take your time here: inhale and rise up on your toes as you turn, exhaling as you rest down onto your heels, looking straight ahead. If you exerted yourself during the sequence, you will need to bring your breathing under control at this point.

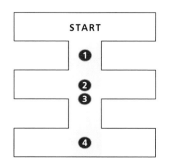

START
1
2
3
4

Taegeuk 8 • *Pal-Jang*

Pal-Jang is the last in the Taegeuk series and is required for candidates testing for 1st Keup (Red belt, black tags). As such, it is the most difficult but, in my opinion, also the most beautiful when performed properly. Many of the techniques are executed from difficult positions so, in order to perform well, a high degree of balance is

*✳ START

Ready stance (*chumbi seogi*)

1a Twist to your right as you prepare both arms to deliver an outer forearm twin mid-section guarding block leading with the left arm.

❶

1b Step forward into back stance with the left foot and execute the guarding block.

2a Withdraw the right fist to your hip and slide forward with your left foot as you prepare to deliver a reverse punch in long stance.

3c Immediately bring your left leg through as you land on your right foot to deliver front kick, and shout (*kihap*). Kick and land with the other foot simultaneously.

3d Withdraw the kicking foot to the opposite knee as you prepare both arms and hips for mid-section inward block using left outer forearm.

3e Step down to form a left-leg long stance and execute the inward block.

Hints and tips

• Make sure that you load your hips sufficiently to perform the blocking action with enough power to be effective, as you step down.

required, as well as the ability to generate a lot of power with less dramatic body action. This sequence involves an additional stance not previously covered nor widely used in other aspects of Taekwondo. Tiger stance (*beom seogi*) is a close-range defensive position, emphasizing weight distribution largely on the rear foot, with both

Hints and tips

• Perform this and the next kick in rapid succession, as though leaping over an obstacle that is placed in front of you.

2b Execute the mid-section reverse punch, thrusting the hips forward as you form long stance with the left foot.

3a Transfer your weight onto your front foot in order to leap up and forward from it.

3b Launching off the left foot, perform a right-leg jumping front kick.

3f Withdraw the left fist and execute a reverse mid-section punch with the right fist, turning the hips to the front.

3g Remain in position as you execute a mid-section forward punch with the left fist.

4a As you draw your rear foot up, prepare your arms and hips for the next right-fist punch.

4b Step into long stance with the right foot and execute a mid-section punch with the right fist.

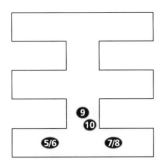

Taegeuk 8 • *Pal-Jang continued*

feet close together, front heel raised off the floor and the knees bent, one tucked in behind the other. Try to get the feeling of sitting in the stance rather than standing over it, but keep your back straight. Here, it is used when performing palm heel block against the front kick, as it offers greater protection in case of a low-section attack.

5a Draw your rear foot up and pivot 270 degrees anti-clockwise, as you prepare for a simultaneous left-arm low block and right-inner-forearm outward block (high-section).

5b Extend your left foot out (backwards) to form a right-leg long stance as you execute the simultaneous blocks, looking over your left shoulder.

6a Begin the turn to face forward as you drop the right fist to your hip and prepare to deliver an upward punch to the chin. Keep the fist turned down, to utilize the wrist rotation in Step 6b.

8a Begin the turn to face forward as you drop the left fist to your hip and prepare to deliver an upward punch to the chin. Keep the fist turned down, to utilize the wrist rotation in Step 8b.

8b Rotate both hips and feet to the front, forming right-leg long stance. Execute a left-fist upset punch, pulling the right fist to the left side of your chest. Perform this in slow motion.

9a Pick up your front foot and turn 270 degrees anti-clockwise looking over your left shoulder and prepare to deliver mid-section twin-knifehand guarding block in back stance.

Hints and tips

• When turning, always lead by pulling your hips through the movement rather than your stepping foot. This will make for a faster and more balanced turn.

Hints and tips

- Keep your knees bent as this is a transitional movement that will place you in the correct position if you step approximately 30 cm (1 ft) across.

6b Rotate both hips and feet to the front forming left-leg long stance. Execute a right-fist upset punch, pulling the left fist to the right side of your chest. Perform this in slow motion.

7a Withdraw your left foot, turning clockwise and stepping over the right leg, and cross your arms to prepare for the combination high/low block to the opposite direction.

7b Step across with the right foot to form a left-leg long stance. Look over your right shoulder and deliver a right-arm low block and left-inner-forearm outward block (high-section).

9b Step down into back stance with the right foot behind, as you execute the guarding block to the front.

10a Drop your right fist to the hip and slide your front foot forward as you prepare to deliver a reverse mid-section punch in long stance.

10b Form left-leg long stance and execute the reverse mid-section punch with the right fist.

11a Transfer your weight onto the front foot and bring your right foot to the left knee to deliver front kick.

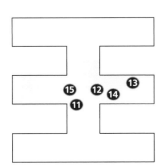

11b Tilt back on your supporting foot and execute a right-leg mid-section front kick.

11c Withdraw your kicking foot to the opposite knee and prepare both arms for a right-arm palm heel block.

11d Step back with the right leg, returning the foot to its previous position, then begin to draw your front foot backwards.

11e Place your left foot behind the right as you form tiger stance, and deliver a right-arm palm heel block.

13b Tilt your upper body back and extend the left hip forward as you execute a left-leg front kick.

13c Withdraw the kicking foot smartly to the opposite knee before stepping down into long stance.

13d Having first dropped your right fist to your hip, step forward with the left leg into long stance and execute a mid-section reverse punch with the right fist.

14a As you withdraw your front foot, prepare both arms for a mid-section palm heel block with the left hand.

Hints and tips

• Don't pause when raising the foot before kicking. This action should be performed explosively as part of the kick itself.

12a Bring your left foot forward and prepare for twin-knifehand guarding block as you turn to face left.

12b Step forward into tiger stance with the left leg and execute the guarding block.

13a Raise the left foot to the opposite knee in preparation for delivering mid-section front kick. Maintain your composure during this manoeuvre.

14b Form tiger stance with the left foot forward and deliver the left-hand mid-section block.

15a Pivot 180 degrees clockwise on your left foot and prepare to deliver twin-knifehand guarding block.

15b Form tiger stance with your right foot forward and deliver twin-knifehand guarding block to the mid-section.

16a Raise the right foot to the opposite knee in preparation for delivering mid-section front kick. Maintain your composure during this manoeuvre.

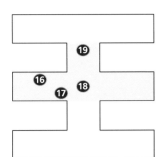

16 b Tilt your upper body back and extend the right hip forward as you execute a right-leg front kick.

16 c Withdraw the kicking foot smartly to the opposite knee before stepping down into long stance.

16 d Having first dropped your left fist to your hip, step forward with the right leg into long stance and execute a mid-section reverse punch with the left fist.

17 a As you withdraw your front foot, prepare both arms for a mid-section palm heel block with the right hand.

18 b Form back stance and execute twin-forearm low-section guarding block.

* FRONT VIEW

19 a Bring your left foot up to the opposite knee and prepare to kick mid-section.

* FRONT VIEW

19 b Tilt your upper body back and extend your hips forward as you execute a mid-section front kick with the left foot.

* FRONT VIEW

Hints and tips

• Ensure that you finish the blocking actions at the same time as stepping into the stance, but do not sacrifice the correct preparation for speed.

17b Form tiger stance with the right foot forward and execute the right-hand mid-section block.

18a Pivot 90 degrees clockwise on the front foot by stepping back with the left leg, and prepare to deliver low-section twin-forearm guarding block.

✴ FRONT VIEW

✴ FRONT VIEW

✴ FRONT VIEW

✴ FRONT VIEW

19c Withdraw the kicking foot to the opposite knee and maintain composure before switching for the next kick.

19d Switch feet and execute a right-leg jumping front kick before stepping down with the left foot, and shout (*kihap*).

19e Step down with the right foot forward and prepare for outer forearm mid-section inward block with the right arm.

19f Deliver the block in a right-leg long stance, rotating the hips left.

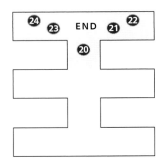

* FRONT VIEW

20a Execute a reverse mid-section punch with the left fist as you rotate your hips to the front.

* FRONT VIEW

*

20b Without pausing, follow up with a forward mid-section punch with the right fist.

21a Pivot on your right foot 270 degrees anti-clockwise to face left, and prepare for knifehand mid-section block with the left hand.

23a Pivot on the left foot 180 degrees clockwise and prepare for knifehand mid-section block with the right hand.

23b Step in with your right leg and deliver the knifehand mid-section block.

24a Slide your front foot forward into long stance and execute high-section elbow strike with the left arm.

24b Immediately follow up with high-section backfist front strike with the same arm.

21b Step in with your left leg and deliver the knifehand mid-section block.

22a Slide your front foot forward into long stance and execute high-section elbow strike with the right arm.

22b Immediately follow up with high-section backfist front strike with the same arm.

22c Complete the combination with a forward mid-section punch with the left fist.

24c Complete the combination with a forward mid-section punch with the right fist.

Look over your left shoulder as you pivot anti-clockwise on your right foot to assume ready stance once more. Again, take your time here, and bring your breathing under control.

* END

Hints and tips

- As always on the turn, ensure that you look in the new direction before moving, otherwise you will be turning blindly into the next position.

Part three
Taking it further

In this final section we address the different types of sparring practised in the dojang. This, along with self-defence practice, also covered here, is the closest you will come to actual combat while still in the training environment. It is vital that you exercise maximum care and control when working with classmates, remembering always that this person is not your opponent but your training partner. Treat them accordingly. The last aspect covered is *kyukpa*, or 'breaking'. Highly enjoyable and rewarding for the early learner, it is a true test of one's maturity in Taekwondo. Only attempt this in the presence of your instructor, and don't be too ambitious, as an injury will set you back in your development for several weeks – if not more.

Sparring

In this section, we look at two different types of sparring that you will practise in the dojang. Sparring is the closest form of exercise to actual combat while remaining in a controlled environment. It involves putting your techniques into practice using real attack and defence movements against a partner, and various sequences are included on the following pages to help you test your skills.

WHEN TO START

This aspect of Taekwondo practice is a very enjoyable and rewarding experience that most beginners look forward to enthusiastically. However, it should not be attempted until you have been practising regularly for a couple of months, as it will take you at least this long to grasp the fundamentals of correct blocking, kicking and striking towards a moving target, without suffering loss of balance or accidentally causing injury through poor control.

The introduction of sparring into your training regime should be progressive, and at a pace conducive to your ability to learn. It would be unwise, for instance, to allow a novice into a free-sparring environment, facing a real and moving opponent, without first giving appropriate tuition on sparring methodology and the application of proper Taekwondo techniques for this situation.

SHIN GUARDS

ONE-STEP SPARRING

The first type of sparring is called *hanbon kyurugi*, or one-step sparring. This is a carefully controlled setting where the purpose is to develop and improve your timing, coordination, balance and speed of reaction when faced with an opponent standing in front of you and trying to strike at you – in this case, with a forefist punch.

First, agree with your partner where the attack is going to be directed (for instance, whether middle section or high section). This is most important in the early stages, as it will reduce the chances of you misreading the attack and receiving a rather unpleasant punch in the face. Your role is then to deflect the attack successfully by blocking and/or moving your body out of the line of attack, and promptly and decisively counter-attacking with minimum delay. (Note: the instructions in each sequence are always directed to the defender.)

HEADGEAR

GROIN GUARD

FOREARM GUARDS

There are no predefined responses to the attack, as the underlying principle is to use your creativity and imagination to react, using Taekwondo techniques according to your grasp and level of understanding. Rehearse as many variations of defence and counter-attacks as you can and you will find that your confidence will improve dramatically as you prepare for the next stage of sparring.

FREE SPARRING

Free sparring brings together all your skills in a free-moving situation. Here you will have certain rules explained to you that will minimize unnecessary and avoidable accidents. These rules will vary according to the level of contact permitted and, hence, protection used by the participants. If the sparring practice employed in your dojang is of a 'non-contact' nature, then there will be far more stringent rules to protect both players. If, however, the practice is to permit touching with the attacks – known as 'contact sparring' – then safety equipment (as pictured here) must be worn by both players (see also *Note on New Competition Rules*, page 144). Gumshields are not mandatory in Taekwondo but may be worn for additional protection.

This aspect of training provides you with the opportunity to practise successive and non-stop Taekwondo techniques in a constantly changing situation. It is the physical expression of all that you have learned, and is a great measure of your inner strength as well as your physical capabilities. Unless you are competing in a tournament where the purpose is to win against the opponent, this is an opportunity to compete against yourself – with the aid of a partner. As always, practise with respect for each other or you will soon run out of partners who are prepared to share this experience with you.

In the beginning, you will find this part of your training difficult as you struggle with what you had previously thought to be a reasonable level of coordination skills. Soon you will become more creative and ambitious as your confidence grows to new heights, and you will want to exhibit progressively more complex and superior techniques. This is when you must take care to listen to your instructor – don't get carried away in the excitement, as this aspect of Taekwondo can be quite harmful if practised unsupervised.

BODY PROTECTOR

One-step sparring

Sequence 1: *Reverse-block/double-punch counter*

We start this section with one of the simpler sequences, to get you used to this type of sparring and the mind-set necessary for the successful application of the techniques. In all the sparring sequences, you are the defender (counter-attacker) receiving the initial attack from your opponent. The instructions take you through your counter-attack step by step. Practise slowly to begin with, ensuring that you adopt the correct distance from your partner.

DEFENDER   ATTACKER

1 Begin in ready stance (*chumbi*), just far enough away from one another to ensure you don't accidentally connect with the target if you mistime your techniques.

2 Your partner steps forward and attacks with a right-fist punch to the face. Step diagonally forward into long stance with your right leg and use a left-arm high block to deflect the attack up and away. Your right arm should be drawn back to your hip in readiness for the counter-attack.

3 Immediately after the block, assume horse-riding stance and rotate your hips around to throw a right high-section counter-punch while withdrawing your left arm to your hip.

Hints and tips

- Timing is essential in one-step, concentrate on making split-second reactions that give no prior warning, otherwise you will be 'telegraphing' your intentions to your opponent.
- If you step correctly in Step 2, you will be in the correct position to change the stance without adjusting your feet (Step 3). Be careful not to over-extend your right shoulder when punching, otherwise you will surely connect with your target.

4 Without pausing, load your hips (by twisting left) before thrusting your left arm out for a middle-section punch. Remember, it's OK to move out of horse-riding stance while between the two punches, as this is necessary in order to generate the required power in your techniques, but make sure you return to the perfect position as you complete the move.

One-step sparring

Sequence 2: *Hook-kick/turning-kick counter*

The defence is a little more complex in this second sequence against the punch, as we now introduce counter-kicks. It is important that you have practised them alone first, as you need to have developed a high degree of control before trying them out on your training partners in the dojang. Again, correct distance and timing are very important to the success of the routine, so begin slowly, checking your position relative to your partner at each stage before adding the speed that will make the sequence effective.

DEFENDER

ATTACKER

1 Begin in ready stance, and at a sensible distance from each other (so that you have a reasonable chance of moving before you get struck by the attack). Remember: you are in a learning environment, so don't make things too difficult for yourself.

2 Your partner steps forward into a right-leg long stance and attacks with a forward mid-section punch. Step back with the right foot into back stance, and defend using a mid-section left-arm inward block.

Hints and tips

- If you slow down on the first kick (Step 3) you will find it more difficult to come back with the second, as you will lose all the momentum of your body spin, so keep your centre of gravity low and concentrate on spinning a full 360 degrees with the hook kick, to land on the same spot as the before.

3 With your weight transferred onto your front foot, look over your right shoulder and spin clockwise, executing a right-leg high-section hook kick. Depending on your distance from your partner, and your own leg length, you may need to adjust your front foot before kicking. If anything, pull it away slightly (as shown here) to prevent the back of your leg hitting the target.

4 Continue spinning through the kick until your foot lands back on the floor behind. Keep your guard raised for your own protection and be ready to bounce off the rear foot again for the second part of the two-kick combination. Make sure that you finish completely side-on to your partner.

5 When you place the kicking foot down, keep the knee soft so that it acts almost like a spring, and immediately bounce back up to execute a mid-section turning kick with the instep of the same foot. Shout (kihap) as you deliver this final move in the sequence.

One-step sparring

Sequence 3: *Knifehand/spearhand counter-strike*

The third one-step sparring sequence deals with open-hand techniques, both for defence and for counter-attack. Practise against the same attacking punch, as this presents less difficulty at this stage of learning. Timing now becomes even more important, as you will be stepping forward into the attack, working against your natural instincts to back away, so (again) begin slowly until you become more confident.

ATTACKER

DEFENDER

1 Begin in ready stance – again, at a realistic distance apart – and familiarize yourself mentally with the first move from your partner. Relax, and be ready to respond with your intended blocking action as soon as you see the beginning of the attack.

2 As your partner executes the right-fist punch with a step, rotate to your right to prepare, and then deliver, a right-hand palm heel block. Slip inside the punch with your right foot, into back stance, as you defend using your hips to throw the block round from right to left.

- Don't begin the sequence too quickly – a step too soon will result in you being struck in the mid-section before your block comes into play. Rather, allow a little more room to begin with, and practise adding speed to the block without compromising the correct action.

- Remember that when you make your counter-attack you must do so quickly and decisively, as a real opponent won't stand still waiting for you to strike back. Once you are comfortable with the sequence, introduce more speed until you can explode into one fluid combination of moves without pausing.

3 Now slide your front foot forward and out slightly to make long stance as you counter-strike using a left knifehand strike to the side of your partner's neck. Try to finish the strike at the same time as completing the stepping action.

4 Immediately withdraw your chopping hand as you change the position of your front foot to form horse-riding stance. As you do this, use your hips to throw the right hand forward, striking at the front of the throat using spearhand thrust. As this is the final move in the counter-attack combination, use your *kihap* here for added power and concentration.

Contact sparring

Sequence 1: *Countering the turning kick*

The mid-section turning kick is one of the most dependable basic attacks in Taekwondo. It is both powerful and fast and, since you will face it many times during your sparring bouts, it is appropriate that we first practise against this attack. Don't forget that there are many options available in answer to each of the attacks shown in the following pages; what we offer here is only one possibility that is dependent upon several factors for success. Try to be creative and explore new and varied sequences of your own. That way, your training partner will not view you as predictable when they throw this kick at you.

ATTACKER   DEFENDER

1 Assume a guarding posture facing your partner, with the left leg forward. Try to remain relaxed, as you will find it easier to respond quickly once you see the attack. Position yourself at a distance from your partner suitable to encourage them to want to use the turning kick.

2 As your partner launches the turning kick from the rear foot, you must drop your left arm down to protect your mid-section. At the same time, step diagonally forward onto your right foot and deliver a right-fist punch to your partner's solar plexus.

3 Connect with your punch at the same time as blocking your partner's kick, so that the force destabilizes them while the kicking foot is still in the air. Don't worry too much about where the kick lands on your arm, as it will inevitably glance upward due to the angle of your block and the fact that you are closing in on your partner.

4 As your partner lands, shaken by your punch, throw your own left-leg turning kick into the rib area beneath the right arm, turning your hips fully over.

Hints and tips

- You may find it helpful to adjust your supporting foot away from your partner prior to kicking if you find that you have insufficient room after the punch. But do it quickly, or you will lose the opportunity to follow up successfully with the kick.
- Watch your partner's eyes in Step 1, as these often betray intentions with a glance at the intended target area just before attacking. You need to be sure that the attack is not intended for your head when you drop the blocking arm.

Contact sparring

Sequence 2: *Countering the hook kick*

Here we move on to more advanced combinations typical of Taekwondo. My advice is to break down each kick and practise it against a pad until you can perform them all together. This sequence features a counter attack using the instep, against a high-section hook kick from your partner. Timing is vital, so you need to be light on your feet and ready to react from the start. When ready, agree with your partner to switch feet, then practise with the opposite legs to ensure that you do not become limited in your ability.

DEFENDER   ATTACKER

Hints and tips

- Don't step back too early in Step 3 or your partner will realize that the hook kick will miss its target and may change their mind, which will be more confusing for you.
- If you are too slow with your counter-kick in Step 4, your partner will have enough time to land and block.

1 Begin by facing each other in a guarding position, left leg forward, at a comfortable distance apart. Your position will need to become more realistic as you improve, so that your sparring partner genuinely believes it is possible to commit to the attack with a reasonable chance of success.

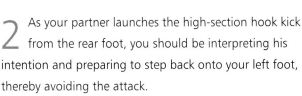

2 As your partner launches the high-section hook kick from the rear foot, you should be interpreting his intention and preparing to step back onto your left foot, thereby avoiding the attack.

3 As the hook kick extends toward you, step back onto your left foot, pulling your hips all the way back. Keep your left knee soft so that you can bounce back from it for your first counter-attack.

4 Immediately you step back, rebound off the rear foot, throwing your left hip forward and executing a mid-section turning kick, connecting as your partner lands from his kick.

5 For the finishing touch to your counter-attack, you need to switch legs quickly. Therefore, as soon as you connect with your first turning kick you must then leap off the supporting foot and change position in mid-air for the follow-up high-section turning kick.

6 Complete your counter-attack combination with the right-leg high-section turning kick. By jumping high enough, you will be able to turn your hips over sufficiently for a powerful kick before landing on your left foot.

Contact sparring

Sequence 3: *Countering the chop kick*

Here your partner has the opposite foot forward to you and this presents them with the opportunity to strike toward your face with a chop kick from the rear foot. Once again, you need to respond quickly and interpret the kick early on in its travel, so make sure that you are fully warmed up and alert when attempting this sequence. You will be countering with a jumping 360-degree turning kick using the instep of your front foot, so correct distancing will be a major factor in the accuracy of this technique.

DEFENDER   ATTACKER

1 Begin with your right leg forward in guarding position, facing your partner, who is assuming a left-leg-forward position. Give yourself plenty of room for this sequence, and only begin closer to your partner when you have practised it a number of times, and are confident in your ability to evade the chop kick.

2 Your partner launches the chop kick from the rear foot. As you see the leg rising, slip your front foot backwards, simultaneously turning 180 degrees anti-clockwise and lifting the opposite leg as though intending to strike with a left-foot back kick. Look over your left shoulder to ensure that you are clear of the descending attack.

3 Before you have turned too far, bend your supporting knee a little more than usual and leap up from it to throw a right-leg turning kick. Continue to spin while in the air and use your left arm to protect against the attack if you are still at risk of colliding with the chop kick.

Hints and tips

- Once you have become sufficiently experienced with the 360-degree spinning action of the kick, replace the step-back of the front foot – and the raising of the left foot – with a simultaneous exchange or 'switching' movement. This will enable you to complete the technique much quicker, giving you a greater chance of success.

4 As your hips come through the centre line, drive your right leg out to your partner's mid-section, connecting with the instep of your foot. If you reacted early enough from the beginning, you will connect just as your partner's foot is landing on the floor. This will make it easier for you to succeed, as your attacker is less able to defend during their kick until they have fully recovered their balance.

Contact sparring

Sequence 4: *Countering the back kick*

This, again, is one of the more complex combinations used by advanced students in Taekwondo. Timing continues to be critical to the success of the sequence, so work on developing your reflexes so that you can respond early to your opponent's attack.

ATTACKER   DEFENDER

Hints and tips

- Don't try to strike too hard with the side kick (Step 2), as you need the resistance of your opponent's body weight to help push off for the next part of the sequence. Instead of trying to score a point with your side kick, use it to 'check' your opponent. Done correctly, and connecting at or around belt level, you will completely spoil your opponent's back kick by upsetting their centre of gravity at a crucial moment in their attack.

1 Begin in a guarding stance with the left leg forward, at a comfortable distance apart. Your partner sees the chance to deliver a right-foot back kick to your mid-section.

2 As soon as your partner turns to launch the back kick, you must seize the opportunity to counter with a mid-section front-leg side kick, thus interrupting your partner's forward momentum. Simultaneously, leap from your supporting leg and begin to turn in a clockwise direction.

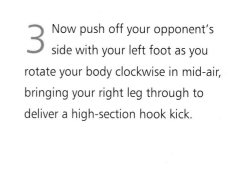

3 Now push off your opponent's side with your left foot as you rotate your body clockwise in mid-air, bringing your right leg through to deliver a high-section hook kick.

4 Use the height gained by the leap to strike high-section with the underside of your right foot while still in the air. Continue the spin through the target to land on the floor in a guarding position, ready for the next attack.

▲ CAUTION

- *This sequence should not be attempted until the basic kicks have been well practised and understood. A high degree of speed and agility is required to accomplish this manoeuvre, so break it down and practise the two kicks separately against a target pad before putting them together.*

- *Due to the complex nature of this sequence, make absolutely certain that your side kick does not become trapped by your opponent, and remains free to withdraw for the hook kick.*

Self-defence *Hosinsul*

This part of your training concentrates on closer-than-usual defence and counter-attack, and is called *hosinsul*. You will need to demonstrate a good understanding of this aspect of training for your Black Belt test, so I strongly recommend that you begin practising early in your training career. Your kicks and blocks are fine when there is sufficient distance between you and your opponent, but when you are grabbed from in close it can sometimes be very difficult to create the room with which to use those techniques. Hosinsul is therefore the answer. Some useful pointers are set out opposite.

Elbow and wristlock from the choke-hold

In this sequence you are confronted with a head-on attack. Though you may initially be somewhat surprised, it is important that you do not hesitate in your reaction. Practise slowly, gradually building speed into your reactions until your response is automatic. Stay relaxed and keep your body upright unless it is your deliberate intention to do otherwise.

1 Your opponent moves in and grabs you by the throat with the right hand, while preparing to punch you in the face with the left fist.

Hints and tips

- By regulating the pressure that you apply to the wrist in Step 2, you can force a submission from your opponent, drive them headlong into the ground, or walk them away.

- Once the wristlock is applied, keep your opponent close to your body or you will lose control and give them the chance to escape your grip.

2 Grasp the attacker's forearm with your left hand to prevent them from releasing, before stepping back with your left foot and turning your body side-on. Bring your right elbow through to strike high-section and place your right hand over the attacker's wrist.

HAND POSITION

Place your right thumb into the centre of the back of the hand, with your fingers wrapped underneath and your left thumb under the wrist. Both hands are now set in position for the release and subsequent wristlock in the next step.

3 Step diagonally out and back with your right foot, then quickly step through to the front with the left foot as you rotate both hands clockwise until you reach your right hip. Apply flexion to the attacker's wrist with your right hand while pressing down by bending your knees and leaning into their arm.

IMPORTANT POINTS TO REMEMBER

- Try to relax rather than tense up, as you will then be able to respond faster.
- Don't hesitate, as this allows your opponent to consolidate their grip.
- Use your opponent's weight to your advantage by moving in the same direction.

- Keep your opponent close to your body. This will help you gain control of the situation.
- Stances are not as vital here. You will be moving from one position to the next very quickly, so keep your steps short and your centre of gravity low to retain your balance.

- Don't focus solely on the hand that takes hold of you, or your opponent may use their free arm or their legs to strike you.
- The instructions below are directed to the defender, but practise as the attacker too, to understand the amount of pressure needed.

Take-down from the handshake

Here you have offered your hand in a greeting but the other person refuses to release your hand despite your attempt to let go. To maintain the grip, your opponent is also pulling on your arm, so you can again turn this into your advantage by pushing forward with your response and throwing your attacker to the floor.

Hints and tips

- By using your left hand to apply flexion to your opponent's hand, you will be able to unbalance them.
- The key to success is the twist outward of your opponent's wrist as you bend their arm up, so concentrate on this part of the movement.

1 Your aggressor refuses to let go but is not showing any indication of wanting to hit you, so a strike is not called for here. Nevertheless, a decisive response is required against this type of intimidation.

2 Step forward with your left foot and grip your opponent's wrist firmly in your left hand, placing your thumb onto the back of the hand. Now you have the strength of both hands against your opponent's one.

HAND POSITION

When grasping your opponent's wrist with your left hand, it's important to place your thumb in line with their fingers and keep it there throughout, as this enables you to control the rest of the movement.

3 To force your opponent to release, simply raise your right arm up in a circular move as though checking your watch. Assist with your left hand and step diagonally forward to the outside of your opponent's right leg. You can now apply pressure to the back of the hand with your right forearm.

4 Continue applying the twist toward the outside of your opponent's shoulder until they begin to fall backwards. Keep your back straight and your opponent close to your body as you control their fall to the floor using the flexion on the wrist.

Release from the strangle-hold

ere your attacker lunges at your throat with both hands. It is quite likely that they will be pushing forward as they attack, forcing you backwards; if this happens, you need to force your opponent off balance as quickly as you can.

By responding immediately, as shown here, you will be able to take control before your upper body is pushed back beyond the vertical position, otherwise it will be considerably harder for you to recover control of the situation.

1 The attacker lunges forward onto the right foot, grabs at your throat with both hands and squeezes. This has the effect of forcing your head back.

2 Resist the urge to step back by transferring part of your weight forward onto your right leg, and strike to the hollow at the base of your opponent's throat using right-spearhand thrust.

3 Immediately after your spearhand attack, place the palm of your right hand on the front of your opponent's chin and your other hand behind their head.

4 Pull round with your left hand as you twist your opponent's head anti-clockwise with your right hand. This will automatically force them to release their hold on your throat.

5 Once your attacker is facing away from you, pull them close to your body and down to the floor without loosening your hold. Keep your back straight by bending your legs as you lower.

6 Continue the twisting motion all the way down, and select your preferred strike to the fallen opponent before making your escape to safety.

> ▲ **CAUTION**
>
> - *Take great care during Step 4. Practise slowly, with no jerky movements, as it is extremely easy to injure your training partner seriously with this technique. Remember the Taekwondo rule: respect your partner at all times.*

Elbow striking against the lapel grab

This is a common attack, which invariably precedes an attack using the head or knee. Your response therefore has to be quick and decisive. As before, it is imperative that you retain your balance at the start, so keep your feet a comfortable distance apart, with your body weight evenly distributed. Here, the emphasis is not on forcing the release of your attacker's grip – in reality, this will happen as a result of your counter-actions, as suggested below.

> ▲ CAUTION
>
> • *Do not strike directly on the ear of your training partner with your open hand, as the pressure caused may rupture the eardrum. Instead, for safety, consider contacting the cheek or face to maintain realism.*

1 Your attacker lunges, grabbing your lapels with both hands, and pulls you forward. The assumption here must be that you are to receive a subsequent strike from either the forehead or knee.

2 Whichever leg your opponent steps forward with, use the opposite hand to strike across the ear in a wide circular action with your open palm, stepping forward at the same time to bring your body round.

3 Continue through by turning your body and driving your hips round further. Your front foot should be between your attacker's feet so that your hip and shoulder almost touch your opponent.

4 Having stepped in, you are now close enough to bend your arm and drive your elbow in the opposite direction, back into your opponent's face.

Breaking *Kyukpa*

Kyukpa is an integral part of Taekwondo training for adults and is used in promotion tests for advanced students as well as exhibitions and Technical Competitions. Breaking is a test of concentration, focus, power, speed and accuracy. For grading purposes it is usually performed with 30 x 30 cm (1 x 1 ft) boards, as they break cleanly and create little mess, although for exhibitions roof tiles or similar may be used. It can be immensely rewarding for the practitioner, as it provides immediate feedback and allows you to evaluate the practicality and effectiveness of your techniques. Do not, however, attempt this practice without first receiving

The set-up

This is an essential part of the process and should not be underestimated. In order to demonstrate your competence, it is important that you have practised sufficiently beforehand and are not about to throw away your chance to impress your examiner or audience through poor preparation. It is vital that you have a full understanding of the exact starting position required for each of the techniques that you are required to perform. Illustrated here is a no-fuss, simple guide to correct positioning that will help you to achieve success. Follow these steps, applying similar principles to other hand and foot techniques, and you will be ideally positioned for optimum performance, without the need to adjust your distance.

The important thing to remember is that you want to be in a position to exert maximum force at the moment of – and through – the impact. You don't want to be shuffling about with your feet as you measure up against the target with your practice technique. This kind of uncertainty mars the presentation of many students during examination conditions. By dropping into the correct position first time, you will be reinforcing positive thoughts in the minds of yourself and those who are judging you at this time.

KNIFEHAND SET-UP

1 Place the knife-edge of your striking hand against the target, with your elbow bent slightly and your shoulders square-on. Stand at roughly 30 degrees to the line of the board, thereby ensuring that your wrist does not connect with the edge of the board when you strike.

SIDE-KICK SET-UP

1 The set-up for the kicks is very similar. For the side kick, stand in front of the board, body side-on, with your fingertips touching the board. As your leg is longer than your arm, this set-up will allow you to kick through the target rather than at it.

advice from your instructor, as there is a very real risk of injury if you are not fully briefed and capable of generating sufficient force to succeed. Board holders must also receive instruction in order to provide stable support – so there's no getting mum or dad to hold a board for you so you can impress friends at home!

2 Now step back onto your right foot into an extra-long back stance that will allow you to turn through into long stance as you strike. Your set-up is now complete; all that remains is to prepare yourself mentally and rehearse the application before smashing the board.

2 Step back with your right leg into guarding position. Now, when you practise the side kick from your back leg, you will reach the board with your knee still bent, allowing the full extension of the leg as you continue the power through the target.

Air breaks

Air breaks, also referred to as suspended breaks, depend principally upon speed for their success. Other physical factors include a small and concentrated surface area of the striking weapon and, of course, no technique would ever be complete without power. Also essential is a positive psychological approach. Under no circumstances must you allow yourself to give way to thoughts of possible failure – either in your preparation or delivery. You must, therefore, make certain of (and be confident in) your ability to perform the chosen technique successfully. Take time over your set-up, as this will give you a valuable opportunity to prepare mentally for the task. Rehearse the strike in your mind from the start position, through impact to the completion of the entire movement, remembering that it is the technique that you are demonstrating, and not a display of uncontrolled strength.

RIDGEHAND STRIKE ▼

Stand in line with the edge of the board, with your ridgehand touching the centre while you step back with your right foot into your stance. A right-hand reverse strike performed in long stance, and utilizing your entire upper-body twist, delivers the power and speed necessary for this technique to be successful.

Air breaks continued

Spinning hook kick

You will need to have achieved a reasonably high degree of flexibility in your hips and legs to get the most from this technique. You must connect cleanly with the centre of the board and with your foot fixed tightly in the foot-sword shape (*balnal*). The spinning hook kick is a spectacular technique when performed properly: if you spin fast enough, connect with the back of the heel and maintain your balance throughout, the broken pieces of board will fly a considerable distance. The 'crack' of the break, coupled with an ear-piercing *kihap*, is enough to impress everyone observing.

Hints and tips

- Before attempting this kick for real, practise hard with a pad to develop your technique. If your foot shape is wrong or weak, you will almost certainly hurt yourself.

▲ CAUTION

- *Be sure to set up your board-holder in such a way that you do not send the broken pieces toward any spectators or club members when you break, or you will risk causing others injury.*

◀ Set up in line with the side edge of the board, then step toward the front face of the board so that you are standing around 15–20 degrees off-line, to ensure that the back of your leg does not interfere with the board at the moment of contact. Remember that you want to hit cleanly with the rear of your heel – any other part of the leg that connects at the same time will push the board away, resulting in failure.

Static breaks

Static breaking requires firm support from the board-holders if you are to meet with success. You can add as many boards to the set-up as you wish, limited only by the power of your technique and the capacity of your assistants to hold them. Make sure that you check all the boards to ensure that the grain of each piece is running in the same direction – you have no hope of smashing them if they are not aligned (you'll need an axe!). Take a deep breath, relax, and gain your composure as you set up. You need to make sure that you are mentally focused and concentrating hard on delivering the appropriate technique *before* you commit to striking the target.

Hints and tips

- Remember to aim beyond the surface of the target and continue releasing your power all the way through the board (or boards).

◀ KNIFEHAND STRIKE

You should already be familiar with the correct set-up for this technique, as shown on page 136. Practise the delivery in slow motion from start to finish. When you are ready to strike, use the full potential of your hip action to reinforce your power. *Kihap* just before you begin to strike, and continue with the yell until you finish.

◀ SIDE KICK

Again, you can refer back to page 136 to check the correct set-up. Kick using the rear foot to use all your available power, and make sure that you fully straighten the leg through the target. Pivot your supporting foot through 180 degrees to allow your hips to move through and into line with your shoulders.

TURNING KICK ▶

Set up at an angle of 45 degrees to the front of the target, thus ensuring that you connect with the ball of the foot rather than your toes. If you are permitted, practise the kick slowly against the target before you strike, making sure that your hips turn through and your knee remains bent at contact.

Glossary

TERMS USED IN THE BOOK

an palmok	inner forearm
ap chagi	front kick
ap chook	ball of foot
ap koobi	long stance
ap seogi	walking stance
arae	low section
arae makki	low block
bakat palmok	outer forearm
bakat palmok geodureo momtong bakat makki	outer forearm twin mid-section guarding block
bakat palmok momtong anmakki	mid-section outer-forearm inward block
baldeung	instep of foot
balkeut	underside of foot
balnal	foot sword
bandae jireugi	reverse punch
baro jireugi	forward punch
batangson	palm heel
batangson makki	palm heel block
batangson teok chigi	palm heel strike
beom seogi	tiger stance
chumbi seogi	ready stance
deungjumeok	backfist
deungjumeok ap chigi	backfist front strike
deungjumeok yeop chigi	backfist side strike
dobok	uniform
dojang	place of training
dollyo chagi	turning kick
dollyo makki	turning block
dwit chagi	back kick
dwit chook	bottom of heel
dwit koobi	back stance
dwitkumchi	back of heel
eolgul	high section
eolgul makki	high block
eotgeoreo makki	cross-hand block
hanbon kyurugi	one-step sparring
hosinsul	self-defence
huryeo chagi	hook kick
Il-Jang	poomsae sequence (Taegeuk No.1)
joochum seogi	horse-riding stance
ju mok	fist
kihap	shout
kyukpa	breaking
kyung ye	bow
momtong	middle section
momtong bakat makki	mid-section outward block
momtong bakat palmok makki	mid-section outer-forearm block
naeryu chagi	chop kick
Pal-Jang	poomsae sequence (Taekgeuk No.8)
palkup chigi	elbow strike
palkup dwit chigi	backward elbow strike
poomsae	patterns/forms
pyeonsonkeut chireugi	spearhand thrust
pyeonsonkeut seweo chireugi	middle spearhand strike
Sa-Jang	poomsae sequence (Taegeuk No.4)
seonkeut	spearhand
sonnal	knifehand
sonnal deung	ridgehand
sonnal mok chigi	knifehand neck strike
Taegeuks	series of eight patterns up to Black Belt
twieo	jumping
yeop chagi	side kick

ADDITIONAL TERMINOLOGY USED IN THE DOJANG

CLASS TERMS

Kwanjangnim	Head of School
Sabumnim	Master Instructor
Kyobumnim	Instructor
Seon banim	Senior student
Jooshim	Referee
Booshim	Judge

TRAINING TERMS

charyeut	attention
shijak	begin
kalyeo	break
keasok	continue
kuman	stop
kyoruggi	sparring
hogul	chest protector
bo hogul	safety gear

COUNTING

hanna	one
deul	two
set	three
net	four
dasut	five
yasut	six
ilgup	seven
yeodul	eight
ahop	nine
yeol	ten

Resources

USEFUL CONTACTS

KOREA
The World Taekwondo Federation
5th Floor, Shinmunno Building,
238 Shinmunno 1st Ga
Jongro Gu
Seoul, Korea 110-061
Website: www.wtf.org

UK
British Taekwondo Control Board (WTF)
11 Hassocks Hedge
Banbury Lane
Northampton
NN4 9QA
England
Website: www.btcb.org

USA
United States Taekwondo Union
One Olympic Plaza
Suite 405, Colorado Springs
CO 80909
USA
Website: www.ustu.org

CANADA
WTF Association of Canada
1300 Carling Avenue
Suite 208
Ottawa, Ontario
K1Z 7L2
Canada

AUSTRALIA
Taekwondo Australia Inc.
24 Orion Street
Vermont, Melbourne
VIC 3133
Australia

FURTHER READING

There are many fine works available by different authors throughout the world, each focusing on the many and varied aspects that make up the complete subject of Taekwondo. But I would like to recommend one, in particular, that stands out in my mind as being especially significant:

Taekwondo: Philosophy and Culture
Professor LEE Kyong Myong 9th Degree
Hollym International Corporation, 2001
(Originally published by Hyung Seul Publishing Co.)

Index

A

ability: natural 28–9
accidents 31
age: to start Taekwondo 28
All African Games 11
ap chagi 78–9
ap chook 45
ap koobi (long stance) 40, 42, 47
ap seogi (walking stance) 40, 42, 46
arae makki 54–5
arm swings 34
attitude 28

B

back bends 35
back of heel 45
back kick 86–7
    countering 130–1
    jumping 87
back stance 42, 48
backfist 45
backfist front strike 53
backfist side strike 52
backward elbow strike 70–1
baldeung 45
balkeut 45
ball of foot 45
balnal 45
bandae jireugi 51
baro jireugi 50
batangson 45
batangson makki 62–3
batangson teok chigi 77
belt:
    colours 22–3
    tying 20, 21
blocks 43, 54–65
    cross-hand 64–5
    high 60–1
    inward 56–7
    low 54–5
    outward 58–9
    palm heel 62–3
body protector 117
bottom of heel 45
bow 13, 19
breaking 23, 31, 136–9

set-up 136–7
breaks:
    air 137–8
    static 139

C

children:
    classes for 16
    technique not to be used by 72
    warm-up exercises 32, 33
choke-hold: elbow and wristlock to counter 132
chop kick 82–3
classes 13
    for children 16
    discipline and conduct 18–20
    finding 16–17
    lesson format 30–1
    levels in 24
    size of 24
clothing 20
    adjusting 20
    protective 116–17
conduct 13, 18–20
contact sparring 117, 124–31
cross-hand block 64–5
crunches 36

D

destruction *see* breaking
deungjumeok 45
deungjumeok ap chigi 53
deungjumeok yeop chigi 52
discipline 13, 18–20
dobok 20
dojang 13
    children's classes 16
    class sizes 24
    discipline and conduct 18–20
    finding 16–17
    lesson format 30–1
dollyo chagi 80–1
double-punch counter 119
drill 40–1
    hip action 40
    moving 41
dwit chagi 86–7

dwit chook 45
dwit koobi 42, 48
dwitkumchi 45

E

elbow strike 68–9
    against lapel grab 135
    backward 70–1
elbow and wristlock from choke-hold 132
eolgul makki 60–1
eotgeoreo makki 64–5

F

falling 31
fingernails 20, 72
fist 44
    backfist 45
foot sword 45
foot techniques 44, 45
forearm guards 117
forward punch 50
free sparring 31, 117
front kick 78–9
    jumping 79

G

glasses 20
grading system 22–3
grading tests 23
Green, Paul 25
groin guard 116
gum shields 117

H

hanbon kyurugi 116–17
hand techniques 44–5
handshake: take-down from 133
headgear 116
heel:
    back of 45
    bottom of 45
high block 60–1
    /knifehand strike combination 61
hip action 40
history 10–11
hook kick 88–9

countering 126–7
    with turning kick 120–1
    jumping 89
    spinning 138
horse-riding stance 42, 49
hosinsul (self-defence) 31, 132–5
Hudson, Hayley 25
huryeo chagi 88–9

I

Il-Jang 90, 92–6
injuries 31
inner power 14
instep 45
instructors 29–30
insurance 17
inward block 56–7

J

jebipoom sonnal mok chigi 61
joochum seogi 42, 49
ju mok 44
jumping back kick 87
jumping front kick 79
jumping hook kick 89
jumping side kick 85
jumping turning kick 81

K

kicks 43
    back 86–7
    chop 82–3
    front 78–9
    hook 88–9
    jumping back 87
    jumping front 79
    jumping hook 89
    jumping side 85
    jumping turning 81
    side 84–5, 139
    turning 80–1, 139
KIM, Dr Un Yong 11
knee bends 38
knifehand 45
    set-up 136–7
knifehand neck strike 66–7
    high block/strike combination 61

Korea: martial arts 10–11
kyukpa 23, 136–9
kyung ye (bow) 13, 19

L

lapel grab: elbow striking
      against 135
leg swings 37
long stance 40, 42, 47
low block 54–5

M

martial arts 10–11
middle spearhand strike 74–5
momtong bakat makki 58–9
momtong bakat palmok makki
    56–7
Mongelard, Charlene 25
motivation 28
moving 41

N

naeryu chagi 82–3
nails 20
natural ability 28–9
neck strike, knifehand 66–7

O

Olympic Games 11
one-step sparring 31, 116–17,
    118–23
outward block 58–9

P

Pal-Jang 91, 104–13
palkup chigi 68–9
palkup dwit chigi 70–1
palm heel block 62–3
palm heel strike 77
partner work 30–1
pikes 36
poomsae 90–1
postures *see* stances
practice 29
protective clothing 116–17
punches:
    backfist front strike 53
    backfist side strike 52
    forward 50

reverse 51
pyeonsonkeut chireugi 72–3
pyeonsonkeut seweo chireugi
    74–5

R

reverse block/double-punch
    counter 118–19
reverse punch 51
ridgehand 45
ridgehand strike 76, 137

S

Sa-Jang 91, 97–103
safety 20
    equipment 116–17
seated stretches 39
self-defence 31, 132–5
self-discipline 18
seonkeut 45
shin guards 116
side bends 35
side kick 84–5, 139
    jumping 85
    set-up 136–7
single-leg squat 38
skipping 41
sonnal 45
sonnal deung 45, 76
sonnal mok chigi 66–7
sparring 31, 116–31
    contact 117, 124–31
    free 31, 117
    one-step 31, 116–17,
      118–23
    protective clothing for
      116–17
    starting 116
    three-step 31
spearhand 45
    counter-strike to
      knifehand 122–3
    middle spearhand strike
      74–5
    spearhand thrust 72–3
spinning hook kick 138
spirit 14
stances 42
    back 42, 48

horse-riding 42, 49
    long 40, 42, 47
    walking 40, 42, 46
static breaks 139
stepping 41
strangle-hold: release from 134
stretches:
    arm swings 34
    back bends 35
    crunches 36
    knee bends 38
    leg swings 37
    pikes 36
    seated stretches 39
    side bends 35
    single-leg squat 38
    waist twists 34
strikes 43
    backfist front 53
    backfist side 52
    backward elbow 70–1
    elbow 68–9
    knifehand neck 66–7
    middle spearhand 74–5
    palm heel 77
    ridgehand 76
    spearhand thrust 72–3

T

Taegeuk 90–113
Il Jang (No.1) 90, 92–6
Pal-Jang (No.8) 91, 104–13
Sa-Jang (No.4) 91, 97–103
Taekwondo:
    aims of 12
    basic rules 20
    benefits of 12
    dangers 17, 18
    discipline 13, 18–20
    history 10–11
    principles 13, 18
    reasons for choosing 12–13
    rules of conduct 13, 18–20
    spirit 14
    starting age 28
    tenets 12
take-down from handshake 133
target areas 42–3
three-step sparring 31

toenails 20
training 28–31
turning kick 80–1, 139
    as counter to hook kick 120
    countering 124–5
    jumping 81

U

underside 45
uniform 20

W

waist twists 34
walking stance 40, 42, 46
warming down 31, 33
warming up 30, 32–41
    for children 32, 33
    drill 40–1
    importance of 32, 33
    length of 32
    routine 32–3
    stretches 37–9
    warm-ups 34–6
World Games 11
World Military Championships
    11
World Taekwondo Federation
    (WTF) 11
World University Championships
    11

Y

yeop chagi 84–5

Acknowledgements

AUTHOR'S ACKNOWLEDGEMENTS

There are so many people who have made it possible for me to accomplish this work. I would like to thank my mother for supporting and comforting me every day as a boy, when I would return home battered and bruised following my daily sparring sessions. My wife, Lindsay, for shouldering the additional strain of managing the family alone while I slaved over the computer night after night. Paul, Hayley and Charlene, for their talented help as models for the illustrations, and Hayley (Cove) for her inspirational design. And, of course, Tessa, whose patience, understanding and guidance inspired me to the end.

EDDISON • SADD EDITIONS

Commissioning Editor   Liz Wheeler
Senior Editor   Tessa Monina
Proofreader   Nikky Twyman
Indexer   Dorothy Frame

Art Director   Elaine Partington
Senior Art Editor   Hayley Cove
Senior Designer   Rachel Kirkland
Mac Designer   Brazzle Atkins

Production   Karyn Claridge and Charles James

Picture Researcher   Diana Morris
Map Illustrator   Lorraine Harrison
Models   Master Kevin Hornsey, Paul Green, Hayley Hudson and
        Charlene Mongelard

Picture credits   Art Directors & TRIP Photo Library: pages 14–15.
The photograph on page 17 is reproduced by kind permission of
Master Kevin Hornsey.

Eddison Sadd would like to thank Nigel Hudson for his assistance at the photoshoots, and SAM Trading of Manchester, England, for supplying the uniforms and equipment used in photography.

NOTE ON NEW COMPETITION RULES
At the time of this book going to press, new competition rules became effective as of 1 July 2002. The legal scoring area in the trunk is now the whole trunk except the spine, and thus the new-style body protectors no longer include circular target areas.